The 1st Armoured Division

An Operational History

By

John Plant

Published by New Generation Publishing in 2013

Copyright © John Plant 2013

First Edition

The author asserts the moral right under the Copyright, Designs and Patents Act 1988 to be identified as the author of this work.

All Rights reserved. No part of this publication may be reproduced, stored in a retrieval system or transmitted, in any form or by any means without the prior consent of the author, nor be otherwise circulated in any form of binding or cover other than that which it is published and without a similar condition being imposed on the subsequent purchaser.

www.newgeneration-publishing.com

New Generation Publishing

*Dedicated to the memory of
the 13th/18th Royal Hussars*

Contents

Preface vii
1 General Considerations 1
2 Early Days 7
3 France 1940 10
4 England 22
5 Tanks in the Desert 25
6 Retreat to Gazala 32
7 The Battle of Gazala 41
8 The Retreat to Alamein 62
9 The Battle of Alamein 79
10 Tunisia 99
11 Interlude in North Africa 111
12 Components of an Armoured Division 113
13 Attacking the Gothic Line 129
14 Disbandment 148
15 Conclusion 150
Appendix 1 151
Appendix 2 152
Appendix 3 155
Appendix 4 158
Sketch maps 161

Preface

The account here offered to the reading public started life as an appendix to the author's e-book, 'Cruiser Tank Warfare', but, as it grew it became plain that it was a book in its own right. Parts of Chapter 3 has been copied from 'Cruiser Tank Warfare' as have parts of Chapter 7.

The 1st Armoured Division has been largely ignored by military authors and no divisional history exists except for this short one. It must be hoped that the publication of this book will spur some author on to close this gap in the vast array of British military writing.

This account is based on the Official Histories and other readily available printed sources, particularly regimental histories, backed up by material from the National Archive. Any source of information beyond these is given in the notes at the end of each chapter.

Chapter 1
General Considerations

A division is a military formation of between 10,000 and 20,000 personnel, it is usually taken as being the smallest unit capable of utilising the combined action of the different arms for independent operations.

A division consists of three main components:

The headquarters, the functions of which are:

> a) *To help the commander and to provide him with the tactical, technical and administrative data required for the formulation of his plans.*
> b) *To take all action required to implement his plans and to ensure the timely issue of his orders to all concerned.*
> c) *To help subordinate commanders and their headquarters.*

The administrative units:
  The RASC column
  Medical units
  RAOC units
  REME, etc.

The fighting troops.
  They will usually be two or three brigades, and as will be seen this was subject to wide variation.

In a study like this one it is too easy to concentrate on the activities of the armoured brigades, ignoring the other troops. This is a mistake.

By the end of the Second World War an armoured division showed the following characteristics:

1. *The armoured division has certain characteristics peculiar to itself and fundamental differences from other types of divisions. Its first characteristic is MOBILITY. The vehicles of the armoured division can carry all the personnel of the division and the full administrative contents of the first and second line transport in one load. Its fighting vehicles and their organic artillery which supports them, possess a high degree of cross-country mobility, as also do the motorized infantry and certain engineer elements. It is by the judicious exploitation of this characteristic that the full power of the division in the battlefield can make itself felt. The wheeled vehicles are, however, tied to the road and tracked vehicles are susceptible to certain types of terrain. The principle handicap to the free use of armour may well be paucity of roads or unsuitability of terrain, or a combination of both.*

2. *The second characteristic of the armoured division is the ARMOUR which protects the bulk of its main fighting vehicles. This gives it comparative immunity to hostile artillery fire, complete immunity to small arms fire and a high degree of protection against anti-tank weapons. In fact, it gives it the power to close with the enemy in circumstances where this might otherwise be impossible. This comparative immunity furthermore gives it a moral ascendancy over the troops against which it is directed, an ascendancy which should be exploited to the full. Its tracks and belly however, are vulnerable to mines and certain parts of its armour are not immune to the heavier anti-tank equipments. The circumvention or destruction of the enemy minefield and the neutralizing or destruction of anti-tank weapons will generally form essential ingredients of the plan, if armour is successfully to close with the enemy. The inevitable race between armour and anti-tank guns tends to increase the weight of many tanks. Although not affecting their cross-country mobility, this characteristic tends to increase bridging, road and rail movement problems.*

3. *The third characteristic of armour is its HITTING POWER. It possesses great fire power, both in its primary tank armament and in the self-propelled artillery which supports it. It is the skilful development of this characteristic which will enable armour to clear the enemy without undue casualties to itself.*

4. *The fourth characteristic of the armoured division is its VULNERABILITY TO AIR ATTACK, particularly its 'soft skinned' vehicles when on the road. In any circumstances, both armoured and unarmoured vehicles are vulnerable to air attack. Although the former have the protection of their armour, which gives them a certain degree of immunity, they are vulnerable to direct hits by both bombs and rockets. The study of all forms of deception and, as a corollary, of concealment, is therefore of the greatest importance.*

5. *The fifth characteristic of the division lies in THE FLEXIBILITY OF ITS ORGANIZATION. It is so organized that it can be fought in groups of varying constitution according to the task in hand. This characteristic gives great tactical flexibility. Its full development requires a complete understanding between all the elements of the division and excludes any tendency towards a set piece or standard grouping.*

6. *The sixth characteristic of the division lies in the complete ability for the exercise of command and control throughout the whole division by WIRELESS. To get full advantage from this demands a high standard of individual training and a balanced appreciation of the necessity for security.*

7. *The seventh characteristic is the DEPENDENCE OF THE DIVISION ON ITS ADMINISTRATIVE ECHELON, particularly for the provision of fuel and replacement of ammunition. The administrative arrangements must be commensurate with the tactical plan; if they are not complete breakdown of the latter may well result.*

These quotes comes from a post-war manual[1]. Quoting it here may seem anachronistic but, in the late 1940's and early 1950's the British army issued a series of manuals that codified tactics and organisation as they were in 1945 and are very useful in reporting the voice of experience and, one could say, the voice of common sense. It is against this template that the performance of 1st Armoured Division can be measured.

This manual assigns several roles to the armoured division:

a) *Offensive operations.*

- *i)* *The rapid approach to contact the enemy.*
- *ii)* *The delay and disruption of enemy advance.*
- *iii)* *The maintenance of the momentum of the attack on a main enemy defensive area which has been partially or wholly broken into by other arms.*
- *iv)* *The break-out and pursuit consequent upon a successful attack by other arms.*
- *v)* *If necessity demands, the participation in a main set piece attack.*

b) *Defensive operations*

- *vi)* *The counter-attack.*
- *vii)* *If necessity demands, the temporary occupation of a sector in a defensive system.*
- *viii)* *The covering of a withdrawal.*

From this list it can be seen that, by 1945, the armoured division was expected to be able to undertake the vast majority of military operations.

Commanding a mobile formation posed problems far beyond those encountered in the Great War, the limiting factor was always the poor radios of the time. As the Wireless Set No 19 became available the command of the armoured regiments became satisfactory but communication, and hence cooperation, with infantry was always poor. This was one reason why British armoured divisions never quite achieved their full potential.

In general it was found that the best method of radio communication was to use regimental nets, that is with all radios on the same frequency except for those of the reconnaissance troop which was on its own frequency with its rear link on the regimental net. Some regiments preferred to have their heavy squadron (Grants) on their own frequency. This was sometimes a necessity due to the frequency range of the American radios. One result of poor radios was the necessity for frequent and lengthy 'O' groups.

The procedure for commanding the armoured brigades was to have two headquarters, the small tactical one well forward, and the main one about five miles to the rear.

When attacking, the armoured brigade Tactical HQ would follow the leading regiment, or leading two regiments if the brigade was advancing 'two up'. The Tactical HQ would consist of:

Command tank – Brigade commander, Brigade Major,
                                              Signals officer
Spare tank
Scout Car – Liaison officer.

The artillery Tactical HQ would accompany the Brigade Tactical HQ:

Command tank – Regimental commander
Bantam – Orderly officer.

For brigade scale operations the artillery batteries should not be placed under the armoured regiments, but this might be done for the initial stages of a breakthrough, as it was at El Alamein. There will be a FOO (Forward Observation Officer) with each armoured regiment, he will be able to bring down fire in five to ten minutes after it has been requested. This is the time lag if the guns are already in action, it will be less otherwise.

The motor battalion Tactical HQ stayed with the brigade tactical HQ as long as its companies were deployed with their armoured regiments:

Armoured 15 cwt truck – CO
Bantam – Regimental Intelligence Officer.

A 'Bantam' was a variety of Jeep. The command tanks and the 15 cwt truck all had two radio sets.

The intellectual basis of the tactics employed by British armoured divisions throughout the war, what may be called 'cruiser tank warfare'[2], was laid down in 1931 with the publication of 'Modern Formations'. In this manual it is stated that:

This chapter is not intended to lay down the details of the employment of the various formations ... since these can only be worked out in actual practice, but rather to indicate the general principles which should be followed.

It can be seen that, during the lifespan of 1st Armoured Division, there was to be significant development in armoured tactics.

Notes
1   'The Armoured Division in Battle, 1952'
2   This has been covered in this writer's e-book of the same name.

Chapter 2
Early Days

The creation of the 1st Armoured Division was a stage in the rather fitful development of British armoured warfare. The inter-war years had seen experimental forces assembled for exercises on Salisbury plain, but these were not permanent units. As the international situation became steadily more uncertain this had to change. In late 1934 the Chief of the Imperial Staff, General Montgomery-Massingberd, decided to set up a 'Mobile Division' to replace the cavalry division in the order of battle for the BEF being planned for deployment on the continent.

The concept of the mobile division was first given a trial in September 1934 then the tank brigade was joined, temporally, by the 7th Infantry Brigade for exercises culminating in the 'Battle of Hungerford'[1]. This exercise seemed, superficially, to have been humiliating for the armoured troops, but shortly afterwards planning for the mobile division was taken a step further. It was to be based on the Tank Brigade and was commanded by General Hobart.

The anticipated establishment of the Mobile Division varied wildly but, on 18th December 1935, when the Army Council announced that the division would be formed as soon as possible its anticipated order of battle, which was never achieved, was:

Divisional HQ
    2 Armoured car regiments
    2 Mechanised cavalry brigades
        1 Light tank regiment
        2 Motorized cavalry regiments
    1 Tank brigade
        1 Light tank regiment
        3 Mixed regiments
    1 Mechanised RFA brigade (later termed a 'regiment')
    1 RFA brigade

1 RE field Squadron
Admin troops

The motorized cavalry regiments were dismounted cavalrymen in trucks.

There were weak points in the planning at this stage. One was the uncertainty over the role of mechanised cavalry. Another was the purpose of the mobile division, which was taken to be the same as that of the cavalry division it was replacing. These roles were: reconnaissance, screening, occupying important locations in advance of the main force and manoeuvring round the enemy's flank. As a result of this uncertainty there was a proposal to remove the tank brigade from the division. This did not happen but the proposal does illustrate the lack of clarity of planning.

The mobile division was not actually established until September 1937, the commander being Major-General Alan Brooke, later Field Marshall Viscount Alanbrooke. This appointment was not that welcome to the army, which wanted a cavalryman, Major-General Blakiston-Houston, as commander, or to the Tank Corps which had several candidates, but in the event worked out well. One reason for this was that General Brooke, whose background was in artillery, sympathised with both the cavalry and the Tank Corps and had the tact to prevent internecine squabbles. More importantly he understood that the tank would always require the support of the other arms, so was able to prevent the Mobile Division drifting into an all-tank establishment as some tankmen wanted.

This organisation was changed in 1939 to:

2nd Light Armoured Brigade (the new name for a
Mechanised Cavalry Brigade)
1st Heavy Armoured Brigade (the new name for the Tank
Brigade) of three mixed regiments
and an even more inadequate Support Group.

The tank brigade had been formed in 1931 on a temporary basis in 1931 but becoming a permanent one in 1934 with its commander the intense Brigadier Hobart. The Mechanised Cavalry Brigade had been formed in late 1938 by converting the Tidworth cavalry brigade. In 1939 there were two further changes when Major-General Evans took over command from Alan Brooke who was promoted to the command of an Anti-Aircraft corps and the title of the Mobile Division was changed to '1st Armoured Division'.[2]

Following the declaration of war, 3rd September 1939, a large number of reserves rejoined their regiments which were fully occupied with reorganisation and basic training. There was little scope for regimental or brigade training, partly because of lack of vehicles, and partly because of an outbreak of foot and mouth disease which limited the space available.

In November the division was deployed guarding the east coast from the Yorkshire Wolds south to Harwich and this did not help training. Fortunately the division was released from this role in January 1940 when it went on a large scale exercise, the conclusion from which was that the two armoured brigades should be the same. Consequently the division's order of battle was changed to that given in the next chapter. 'Heavy' and 'Light' were dropped from the titles of the armoured brigades, and the 1st Armoured Brigade became the 3rd. This change may well have looked good on paper, but all it really meant was that 3rd Armoured Brigade gave up half its Cruisers to the 2nd Armoured Brigade. Unfortunately there was no time for this new configuration to be tested in any major exercises before the division was deployed to France.

Notes
1   This exercise is described in this author's 'Cruiser Tank Warfare'.
2   Presumably records of this change have been lost, this author could not find them.

Chapter 3
France 1940

At the start of the Second World War the BEF was sent to France. Compared to 1914 this was a leisurely deployment, particularly, although there is of course no direct comparison, in terms of armour. All three types of armour were involved. There were armoured reconnaissance regiments, some comprising armoured cars, and others light tanks and carriers. Infantry tanks were to make up the 1st Army Tank Brigade which, because of the low rate of tank production, was to consist of only two battalions, the second arriving in May 1940. Cruisers would be deployed in the armoured division.

The 1st Armoured Division, commanded by Major-General R Evans, with its Cruiser and Light tanks, was an essential part of the BEF, but its deployment was a huge exercise in muddling through. As Field Marshal Earl Kitchener commented about an earlier war, '*We had to make war as we must, not as we would like to do.*' It started to arrive in France just after the second Infantry Tank battalion. The deployment was rushed and the division was short of many things, particularly artillery and radios, both for its HQs and tanks. It was never to fight as a division.

The state of the tanks was worrying. The latest mark of Cruisers, A13, had only just been issued and the crews had not trained on them. Worse, the machine guns, new BESAs, and some of the 2-pdrs, only arrived just as the units were embarking. The guns that were still in their packing cases were covered in mineral jelly, and there was little cotton waste to clean it off with. After disembarkation the guns were mounted on the tanks, but there was no opportunity to zero them on a range. This was important for the 2-pdrs as, although the guns could be bore-sighted to line up with the sights, the location of the recoil buffers, above the barrels, caused the guns to fire a little low. So the first round was apt to fall short.

A further complication was that the .5-inch ammunition, required for some of the light tanks, was issued loose and had to be loaded into steel-link belts by hand. There was a shortage of 2-pdr ammunition and smoke grenades. All this, and more, was not helped by the internal lights on some of the tanks not working.

The division looked impressive on paper:
1st Armoured Division – Major-General R Evans
    2nd Armoured Brigade – Brigadier RL McCreery
        The Queen's Bays
        9th Queen's Royal Lancers
        10th Royal Hussars
    3rd Armoured Brigade – Brigadier JG Crocker
        2nd Royal Tank Regiment (2RTR)
        3rd Royal Tank Regiment (3RTR)
        5th Royal Tank Regiment (5RTR)
    Support Group – Brigadier FE Morgan
        Two infantry battalions
        101st Anti-Tank/Light Anti-Aircraft Regiment

The two AT batteries of the artillery regiment were each fully equipped with twelve 2-pdr AT guns, but the AA batteries had had to leave their 40-mm Bofors guns in the England. They were replaced by 96 Lewis guns. This was a significant loss to the division, the Bofors were not only excellent AA guns but, in 1940, were quite reasonable AT guns.

However even before the entire division had embarked for France the infantry of the Support Group and a Tank battalion, 3RTR, of 27 Cruisers and 21 light tanks, were detached and sent to Calais. They were permanently lost to the division, which finally deployed a total of 143 Cruisers and 114 light tanks, and no field artillery.

The leading troops had started landing at Le Havre on 15th May, but as that port was under attack from the German Air Force, the rest of the division was diverted to Cherbourg where it started to land on the 19th. It was to be placed, off and on, under French orders and was presently joined by the 51st Highland Division and some *ad-hoc* units. These formations fought a campaign entirely separate from that which ended at Dunkirk, and which, remarkably, has been largely ignored ever since. *(see Sketch 1)*

The division was initially instructed to take up a defensive position along a sector of the Somme, downstream from Amiens. Unfortunately the Germans had already established four bridgeheads across this river, and, in line with their standard procedure, had set to to make them tank-proof. Consequently it was decided to send the AA and AT regiment and the first available armoured regiment, the Bays, to the north of the Seine to take up a position to the east of Rouen to defend the line of the Andelle. This river runs north-east from the Seine and if it could be defended would prevent the Germans getting behind the troops on the Somme.

The Bays and artillery were transported by rail to the Seine and were on the Andelle in the pouring rain on the 22nd. Next day the Bays were moved by General Evans to the line of the Bresle which runs parallel to the Somme, about 15 miles behind it. An order was received from the War Office to attack across the Somme, advance North-East to link up with other British units whose locations were a little vague. Not only was there this vagueness, but the French, with whom the armoured division would have to cooperate, had a basically different view of what it would do.

Fortunately the rest of the 2nd Armoured Brigade had landed and joined the Bays on the 24th. Like the Bays the two regiments were brought most of the way by rail, but still had to cover 65 miles on their tracks in 24 hours to be in time for the fighting. Doing so they passed the sobering sight of the remains of a refugee column that had been machine-gunned from the air. The brigade was given three companies of the 4th Battalion, the Border Regiment, and took the armoured division's artillery regiment and some engineers under direct command. The Border Regiment battalion was a lines of communication unit and was not intended for front line service, but played its part as well as any.

The advance guard of the brigade, provided by the Bays, approached the Somme early in the morning. It lost two tanks on mines and found that all the crossings were mined and guarded. Attacks on three bridges were ordered, each undertaken by a company of the Border Regiment supported by tanks of the Bays. All the attacks failed and lives were squandered pointlessly.

That night orders were received from HQ BEF to delay independent operations and be ready to cooperate with the French. Soon afterwards a message was received from the French to the effect that the 51st Highland Division was arriving from the Saar front. It was to be grouped with the armoured division and the resulting formation would hold the Somme from Longpre to the sea. Until this happened the 1st Armoured Division should eliminate the German bridgeheads. This was beyond the capacity of the division. Not only were the Germans steadily reinforcing their positions on the Somme, but they were patrolling forward, sometimes with armoured cars, as far as the Bresle. On 25th May the division came under the orders of the French 7th Army, and the next day it was to support the French attack on the Abbeville bridgehead.

By this time the depleted 3rd Armoured Brigade had come up. The two armoured brigades were parcelled out separately each to support a French light cavalry division (DCL), still partly horsed. The 2nd Armoured Brigade, with the 2nd DCL, was to capture the high ground south of the Somme immediately south-east of Abbeville. The 3rd Armoured Brigade, with 5th DCL, was to capture the high ground covering the Somme north-westwards to the sea. The French were to supply artillery and infantry, the British the armour, but with the language difficulties and the lack of time for rehearsals, the prospects of success were, to say the least, slim.

The action was ordered for the 27th May, but General Evans was not pleased with this plan, telling the French army commander that Cruiser and light tanks were not suitable for this kind of deliberate assault, but to no avail. It is possible that the French had heard about the Arras counter-attack and were expecting the armoured division's tanks to be Matildas. The action was not a success. The 2nd Armoured Brigade, on the right, advanced with the Bays on the right and 10th Hussars on the left and 9th Lancers in reserve. It suffered heavily from AT fire in fortified villages with which the Germans had extended their Abbeville bridgehead. Some AT guns were sited to catch the British tanks as they came over ridges, a tactic which kept ranges short and time for tank commanders' and tank gunners' target acquisition short. All this was made worse by the heavy rain that made the ground sticky and misted up sights. The time of the attack was put back an hour but this message did not reach the 10th Hussars, the dispatch rider having been killed and attempts to pass the message by radio failed. This regiment advanced without infantry or artillery support and was quickly shot to pieces. A single 37-mm AT gun was credited with knocking out nine of the 20 tanks the regiment lost. The Bays attacked at the correct time with artillery support, but still lost 16 tanks. As a result the 2nd Armoured Brigade made no real progress.

The 3rd Armoured Brigade met less resistance and was able to take up positions overlooking the Somme for the loss of 18 tanks. But the French infantry, which should have been supporting the tanks, dug in at least three miles to their rear, forcing the tanks to withdraw.

By the end of the day the division had lost a total of 65 tanks knocked out by the Germans, and 55 tanks with mechanical breakdowns. Two days later, after the 51st (Highland) Division had driven the Germans back a little, many of these tanks were recovered, and the workshops, which had been set up close to Rouen, worked impressively although there was a dire shortage of spare parts. In particular there was a shortage of brake linings for the cruisers, and without them these tanks were difficult to manoeuvre and easier targets for the

Germans. It is possible that there would have been fewer battle casualties if smoke ammunition had been issued, but this was amongst the equipment that the division arrived in France without.

The French infantry, without the British tanks, renewed the attack the next day, but they were no more successful. The vehicle casualties in 2nd Armoured Brigade had been so heavy that the Bays and the 10th Hussars were amalgamated to form a composite squadron which was added to the 9th Lancers to form the 'Composite Regiment'. The 3rd Armoured Brigade was sent back to Rouen to refit. There can be little doubt that the tank losses along with the views expressed to the French Army commander by General Evans about the capabilities of Cruiser tanks resulted in little further use being made of the division by the French. This one action had gone a long way towards destroying the armoured division.

After the unsuccessful infantry attack the French 4th Armoured Division, commanded by General de Gaulle, arrived and on 29th May, and the next day, it attacked in the Abbeville direction, and had some success on the first day. It seems that the failures were due to poor infantry/tank cooperation. However de Gaulle certainly impressed Brigadier McCreery who admired his use of dismounted tank officers as liaison officers and commented '*General de Gaulle's verbal orders for his attack on the 28th May were decisive and clear and inspired everyone with confidence.*' Brigadier McCreery was to be one of the finest senior officers of the war. Perhaps he learned a lot from his brief contact with de Gaulle.

While these French operations were continuing, the 51st Highland Division arrived and put in a limited counter-attack. It and the 1st Armoured Division became the IX Corps of the French 7th Army. As neat as this organisation looked, the British division commanders were as likely to receive orders from British sources as they were from the French.

There was now a short pause in operations. The Support Group lost the Borderers but gained the 2/6th East Surrey Regiment and ten 40-mm Bofors AA guns arrived at last. The 3rd Armoured Brigade took over seven Matildas which happened to be in the area, nominally a part of 1st Tank Brigade. To some extent this set up what remained of the division for the next phase of operations. Meanwhile the divisional workshops were moved to Foret de Louviers, south of the Seine, but a train which had been planned to take the crippled tanks there never materialised so they had to be either towed or abandoned.

The Dunkirk evacuation was complete so there was no longer any requirement to drive north to link up with the troops there. The strategy now was to create a strong front to seal off the area captured by the Germans, and ultimately to advance north from it. The British contribution was to hold the line of the Somme from Abbeville to the sea, which involved having troops on the Bresle and the Andelle. Parts of this line were held by the 51st Division with the Composite Regiment and Support Group under command. It had two brigades along the Somme, and one on the Bresle with the Composite Regiment to its right rear. The 3rd Armoured Brigade deployed along the Andelle but was so understrength that a squadron of the Bays was lent to it.

The French decided to renew the assault on the Somme bridgeheads on 4th June. The main thrust of the attack was to be mounted by the French to capture the high ground overlooking Abbeville. An infantry and an armoured division were to be used and the 51st Division would support them. The operation did not fare well. The Germans had had time to lay AT minefields and prepare their field artillery to engage tanks. When the French troops were recalled, only six out of 30 heavy tanks returned, and 60 out of 120 light tanks. It was plain that there would be no quick French recovery. The fighting caused heavy casualties among the British infantry, fortunately British tanks were not involved.

The Germans, now free of the Dunkirk operation, attacked followed the next day. The 51st Division was pushed beck to the Bresle, its situation would have been worse but for a counter-attack put in by the Composite Regiment. The Germans actually had little reason to attack the Highlanders front, their main assault was to the British right in the direction of Rouen. Two panzer divisions and several infantry divisions were making excellent progress in that direction, and Rouen had the last bridge over the Seine before the sea.

There was an obvious necessity to withdraw the troops holding the Bresle and Andelle behind the Seine, but General Weygand, the Supreme Commander, vetoed this. As the situation became hourly more desperate there was another change in the chain of command. 1st Armoured Division came directly under General Altmayer, commander of a group of 7th Army divisions. General Evans spoke directly with him and agreed that his division would counter-attack to strike the flank of the German advance and prevent them outflanking the Bresle position.

At this time the division, still without the 2nd Armoured Brigade Composite regiment and Support Group, consisted of the 41 Cruisers, 7 Infantry tanks and 31 light tanks of the 3rd Armoured Brigade, and six light tanks of the Bays, probably a small number of light tanks of the 10th Hussars, and some lorry-borne personnel of the Hussars, which was all that was left of 2nd Armoured Brigade.

The counter-attack order was countermanded by General Weygand who insisted that the armoured division should defend a ten mile stretch of the Andelle to cover Rouen. General Evans had to recall his troops, the most advanced of which were in contact with German reconnaissance units. His force, missing infantry and artillery, particularly AT guns, was not well suited to such a defence, but fortunately there were British infantry of another division on hand. The light tanks of the Bays, supported by the Infantry tanks, covered the river crossings while the rest of the armoured brigade pulled back from the river.

The desperate nature of the Allies' situation is illustrated by the increasingly bizarre command arrangements. There were three major British units involved: the Highland Division, the Armoured Division and the Beauman Division. This last was an *ad-hoc* formation made up of lines of communication troops which, in the circumstances, functioned quite well and some of its units were posted along the Andelle. Each of these units reported to different senior French officers. This was a mess that General Weygand does not seem to have been able to sort out.

The Andelle could not be defended against a serious attack. The front was too long and the AT weapons available too few. The river itself was not a serious obstacle to infantry. The Germans employed a *ruse de guerre* and broke through with captured French tanks. The Composite Regiment with the Support Group had just been returned to the Armoured Division. They were taking up their positions to the left rear of the Andelle when they ran into the advancing Germans. Both sides suffered losses, but the British had to pull back. There was now no possibility of restoring the situation by a counter-attack. Soon the Allies were in disarray. The 51st Division was cut off and the Armoured Division crossed the Seine, amid scenes of chaos and confusion, mostly on the 8th of June. On the morning of the 9th the Germans entered Rouen and all the bridges over the Seine were down.

The effect of this was decisive. The 51st Highland Division with the rest of IX Corps was outflanked and surrounded, but its reduction did divert the Germans from attacking across the Seine and so gave the Armoured Division a short while to sort itself out but this was of little advantage. Next day, 10th June, the Germans crossed the Seine and established a strong bridgehead at Vernon. Fortunately they swung away towards Paris which gave the 1st Armoured Division a brief respite during which General Alan Brooke had taken over command of the British troops in France and decided to return them to

England. Consequently on the 16th the remaining tanks of 2nd Armoured Brigade were loaded on a train which trundled off never to be seen again, at least by 1st Armoured Division soldiers. Next day a report was received that the French had requested an armistice. It was all over so the 26 tanks, 11 scout cars and 49 troop-carrying lorries of the 3rd Armoured Brigade drove the 200 miles by road to Cherbourg where they were evacuated. Only nine Cruisers made it back to England out of the 170 that left. This impressive move on tracks was something of an answer to the critics of British tank manufacturers, but there is little doubt that this campaign had shown up the disadvantages of dividing medium armour into two types.

That ended the campaign.[1] It is easy to imagine that, once the hectic pace slowed and the senior officers had a night's rest, they would have reflected on the importance of a simple chain of command, and on the general difficulty of Cruiser Tank Warfare.

It is interesting to consider the effect that a fully manned and equipped armoured division operating between the Somme and what was to be the Dunkirk perimeter might have had on the Germans. However it should be borne in mind that it would have been difficult to supply a division there. Its main port, Le Havre, was within range of German bombers, and the bridges over the Seine and the Somme could have been attacked by dive bombers. Also its tanks, light and Cruiser, were vulnerable to the German 37-mm AT guns. The Arras counter-attack worried the Germans so much because the infantry tanks were not vulnerable to these guns.

Soon after his return to England General Evans recommended a substantial increase in the infantry and artillery component of an armoured division. This was totally unacceptable to the Armoured Corps which took the view that a balanced formation would be at the mercy of a tank-heavy one, and anyway the part played by the 1st Armoured Division was not really an example of Cruiser Tank Warfare, the division never having been deployed as a single unit. The success of Operation Compass, the Wavell offensive against the Italians, seemed to confirm the Armoured Corps point of view.

Keeping the tanks concentrated came to be a basic tenet of Cruiser Tank Warfare though the concept was only lightly mentioned in 'Modern Formations':

'The armoured fighting vehicle acts by fire and movement with the immediate object of creating an opportunity for decisive action and the ultimate one of securing a concentration of superior force at the decisive point.'

The operations in France showed how difficult maintaining this concentration could be. The Armoured Corps developed a dread of deploying in 'penny packets'[2], though if the requirement is to stiffen an infantry defence this kind of deployment can be highly effective.

Throughout the campaign it is difficult to see what alternatives General Evans had to the actions he took. Nevertheless the failure of this campaign seems to have effectively finished his career. It was different for his brigadiers. All three were to achieve high rank during the war.

Some of the 2nd Armoured Brigade's tanks came to light in 1945. They had been used as hard targets on a German tank range.

Notes

1 Not quite the end of the campaign. Due to circumstances now obscure one British tank turned up at St Nazaire, but it had to be left in France. It is to be hoped that the crew were not victims of the Lancastria disaster.

2 *'Penny packets'*, an expression beloved of those writing about tank warfare, but not used by anyone else, seems to be an anglicization of *'en petits paquets'* first noticed, in this context, in *'Taschenbuch der Tanks, Erganzungsband 1927'* by F Heigl.

Chapter 4
England

The bulk of the division disembarked at Plymouth and reformed in the Warminster area. Then, in July, the division except 2nd Armoured Brigade, moved to Surrey to form the mobile reserve covering South-east England. The 3rd Armoured Brigade was sent to Thursley camp, six miles south-east of Farnham and the support group to south of Dorking. However the 2nd Armoured Brigade reequipped only slowly, this was a particularly thin time in terms of equipment and many troops spent long days practicing infantry tactics on Salisbury Plain for want of tanks to train on.

In October the 2nd Armoured Brigade, now at least partly equipped with tanks, moved to Surrey in billets around Hindhead to the south of 3rd Armoured Brigade. In February 1941 the 10th Hussars were visited by the Prime Minister and they put on a display on tanks which finished up with a traditional cavalry-type charge. The regimental history commented that, although this type of tactic might seem appropriate for tanks armed with the short ranged 2-pdr, it would prove inadequate in North Africa.

Around this time Major-General Norrie took over the division from General Evans, and Brigadier Briggs took over 2nd Armoured Brigade from Brigadier McCreery. Under the new brigade group organisation each armoured brigade was to have an infantry battalion. 2nd Armoured Brigade received 1st Rifle Brigade, but it seems that this establishment change did not reach 3rd Armoured Brigade. This was far from the more balanced organisation suggested by General Evans who wanted a full infantry brigade. However General Norrie, whose star was now in the ascendant, believed that a balanced division, like a panzer division, would be at the mercy of a more tank-heavy one, so the British armoured division remained tank-heavy.

3rd Armoured Brigade lost 3RTR in France, and on returning to England, when the two armoured regiments each comprised only one composite squadron with its tanks, it reassembled at Camberley. In August 2RTR was sent to North Africa to join 7th Armoured Division for its Beda Fomm campaign. The brigade then received 3rd Hussars and 6RTR but no infantry battalion. All this happened on a very tight time table as 2nd Armoured Division was sent to North Africa in November 1940 and 3rd Armoured Brigade was swapped to that division in exchange for 22nd Armoured Brigade which was judged to not yet be fully trained. This turned out to be a disaster for 3rd Armoured Brigade which was caught in Rommel's first offensive, however it can be presumed that at the time the brigade was very pleased to be selected to go overseas.

The 22nd Armoured Brigade was composed of yeomanry regiments, and its arrival was popular as all the armoured regiments were now cavalry. The recently arrived reconnaissance regiment was the 12th Lancers. Equipment was improving but slowly, and 1st Armoured Division was, in this respect, the most fortunate of the armoured divisions, yet in January 1941 it had only 70% of its establishment of tanks, and many of these were obsolescent light tanks.

The winter saw some large-scale exercises, some conducted by General Montgomery. In January each regiment went to Linney Head in South Wales to use the ranges, followed by squadron training after which a large proportion of the tanks was taken from the regiments and sent to the Middle East.

In May-June the division moved to the Marlborough area where it was issued with new tanks and undertook intensive training, but in July it lost all its tanks for a second time. It was then ordered to mobilise for service overseas.

Due to a shortage of shipping the whole division could not travel to Egypt in one lift, and 22nd Armoured Brigade went first, in August, from the Clyde, Liverpool and Avonmouth. This brigade had been rushed out for the Crusader offensive, the reason why its tanks had been withdrawn earlier. The brigade was to come under 7th Armoured Division and its first action in the desert was to prove disastrous which may indicate that its training in England was poor.

When the brigade arrived in Egypt it was met by Lieutenant-General Norrie who had been promoted to command XXX Corps, Major-General Messervy took over 1st Armoured Division.

Chapter 5
Tanks in the Desert

As the greater part of the operational history of the 1st Armoured Division was spent in the North African desert this short chapter will consider the tactical implications of fighting in this environment.*(see Sketch 2)*

The Terrain
Most of the actions to be considered were carried out in classic desert conditions. The ground was flat and hard so that vehicles, both tracked and wheeled, could be driven anywhere as required though the pattern was different to the north. On a line running roughly east-west, and about five miles south of the Tobruk perimeter there was a series of ridges or escarpments. These are not high but their northern faces are steep enough to be impassable to vehicles except at a small number of places. There are three escarpments, one on each side of the Trig Capuzzo, an old arab track, and the third roughly three miles to the south so that the southern two escarpments were each side of the Sidi Rezegh airfield. A modern road, known then as the Via Balbia, runs to the north of the ridges, close to the sea. North of the ridges the country is much more broken, and difficult for tanks. Although many map features are actual geographical features, there are many others, like Gabr Saleh, which are only expanses of sand making navigation sometimes very difficult.

Tactical Implications
The open nature of the terrain resulted in surprise being difficult to obtain, and when surprise was achieved it was usually the result of a lapse on the part of the defenders. Naturally deception was taken very seriously but reconnaissance, both ground and aerial, undertaken by both sides was disappointing.

The range of engagement, heat haze, mirages and dust, frequently made AFV identification difficult. The radios of the time were affected by dust, and their poor quality made reconnaissance less effective than it should have been. The radios of the time had only enough range for voice communications within the squadrons or back to RHQ. For transmission back to brigade it was necessary to use morse code. This slowed everything down and gave commanders the opportunity to ignore orders they did not agree with, saying they were not received [1]. The difficulties of navigation made the resupply of fuel, ammunition and rations to the fighting units unreliable and a perpetual worry for the commanders.

Remarkably British tank units were usually better than the Germans at desert navigation. This was because of the use of sun compasses fixed on the turrets. The Germans rejected them because they were too complicated and did not work between 10.0 am and 2.0 pm, but they made great efforts to supply each soldier with a pocket compass. British maps were far better than the Italian maps the Germans had to rely on at the start of the campaign. To compensate for all this the Germans made more use of light reconnaissance aircraft. In general, if the Germans made a mistake, it was a bigger one.

The two airforces provided little direct ground support during the period in question. The lack of landmarks caused difficulties, but the main problem with the RAF, was that a workable system for controlling ground attack aircraft had not been set up - a case of culpable negligence. The RAF did, though, by shooting down a number of Stukas prevent Axis ground attack. German aircraft sometimes machine gunned British tanks, but that was to indicate their position to German tanks. German AA artillery could provide little assistance in the fight against the RAF. Most of its guns were in use in the AT role.

The supply of fuel was made critical by the vast distances travelled by the tanks. The British army supplied petrol in four gallon cans. These were made of welded thin sheet steel. They were referred to as 'flimsies' because of their tendency to split and leak. They were usually packed in wooden crates, two to a crate. This did not always improve things as nails in the crates could sometimes puncture the cans. It has been estimated that 30% of the petrol sent to the troops in the desert was lost because of leaking flimsies, and the vehicles delivering it were sometimes wet with petrol, increasing their already worrying vulnerability. The flimsies were made locally in Egypt, presumably as an economy measure. On the other hand the Germans (Jerries) preferred not to waste fuel like this and used the more solid 'Jerrycan' (*Wehrmachtskanister*). This was a robust 20 litre pressed steel container, with a neck so that it was easier to use without a funnel. It is still in service in most armies today.

Because of the perceived requirement for Passive Air Defence, British formations went into leaguer or 'laagered up'[2] widely dispersed, both within the brigades and one brigade from another. This could make the passing of orders and assembling forces for action difficult.

A further implication of the wide-open spaces was the large frontages covered by the armoured brigades. Tanks were supposed to deploy 100 yards apart. Consequently a regiment advancing with two squadrons 'up' and deployed in extended lines would have a frontage of approximately 3,000 yards. A brigade with two regiments up would cover 6,000 yards. Such, of course, was an imposing sight which commanders in the subsequent Tunisian and Italian campaigns would never see. The photogenic nature of the desert campaigns no doubt played a major part in making them popular with the public and historians. Unfortunately this wide dispersion and the dust inevitably thrown up by moving tanks made the units difficult to control, and difficult for them to generate heavy firepower contributing to the indecisiveness of desert fighting, and British tanks had to learn to drive more slowly to avoid creating dust clouds.

Artillery was, as usual, the God of War. As the surface of the desert was, under a thin layer of sand, hard rock the explosion of shells was more lethal that it would be in Europe. There was not the soft soil to dampen the explosion, instead, the rock provided extra fragmentation. The same facts of geology naturally made it difficult for infantry being shelled to protect themselves by digging in. Conversely the open nature of the desert, the lack of reference points and frequent poor visibility made the application of fire more difficult. Also as soon as the guns opened fire they raised clouds of dust, giving their positions away and inviting counter-battery fire.

The Germans had a great advantage in artillery terms. Their Panzer IV could deliver significant HE fire. The British were particularly vulnerable to HE fire because their AT guns, the 2-pdrs, were rather tall and difficult to conceal and shield. Also their Cruiser tanks were vulnerable because of their thin armour. German tanks would usually not attack until their target had been given a good pounding with HE.

German artillery was usually kept concentrated under a single commander, particularly the medium guns, whereas the British artillery was scattered among the divisions. In general the German artillery can be regarded as the more effective, the more so as the British 25-pdrs were often pressed into doing duty as AT guns, being taken away from their normal role. When considering armoured warfare it is easy to forget what a battle winner a concentrated artillery barrage could be.

Finally there were the climate and the weather. The days were hot, there tended to be a two hour break at noon due to the distortion of vision caused by the shimmering heat, but the nights were cold. This came as a shock to the most recently joined troops. Worse, during what passed for the winter months, it could rain heavily. This reduced visibility, grounded aircraft, made going difficult, particularly for wheeled vehicles, and made life miserable for the soldiers. Tank crews stowed their bed rolls and blankets on the outside of their tanks so they became sodden and cold and the little sleep the crewmen got was rendered less comfortable. Lack of sleep ultimately results in a decline in daytime performance.

The change of season naturally resulted in a change of weather. In summer the days were longer and the heavy rains stopped, but now there were frequent sandstorms. These storms were based on the seasonal wind, the *Khamsin*, the name of which was derived from *chamsoun*, the Arabic for fifty, and this, probably coincidentally, was the approximate time in hours they lasted. They were extremely unpleasant and made movement impossible.

The British and German armies took a basically different approach to nights, and the Germans used them much more efficiently than did the British. The British procedure was at nightfall to 'laager up'. They concentrated their tanks, filled the tanks with fuel and ammunition, had a meal and a night's rest. Shortly before dawn they deployed into tactical formations. The Germans, however, stayed in tactical formation all night, moving as necessary. Their recovery teams scoured the desert for knocked out vehicles and often worked on them *in situ*, providing light by sending up flares. The consequence of this was that the British often knew where the Germans were, but they seldom took advantage of this.

Because of the general remoteness of the battlefields and the lack of scavengers the knocked out tanks and guns, and corpses, would remain *in situ* almost indefinitely. For example the 10th Hussars lost heavily at Saunnu in January 1942, almost exactly a year later the course of operations brought the regiment back to the same location where they buried the desiccated corpses. Also, of course, mines in the desert could stay dangerous for ever even though most were exposed by the wind after a few weeks. They were still being discovered 25 years later.

Many Arab place names include a description and this can make maps easier to understand. A short list of such names may be seen in Appendix 1.

Tactics
Because of their belief in the cooperation of arms, the Germans manoeuvred as complete panzer divisions, masses of vehicles moving slowly, at the pace of the slowest artillery tractor. This could present a very intimidating sight. Conversely the British armour, manoeuvring by brigade or individual regiment, moved much faster, but lacked the punch. Because of the lack of natural obstacles it was difficult to inflict crippling casualties on a tank force, the losing side could always retreat. For the same reason it was almost impossible to envelop an armoured force.

Both sides were to find that, in desert conditions, once a division was broken up it was very difficult to reunite, largely because of the poor radios, but on the other hand inhibiting independent brigade actions could result in tactical opportunities being lost.

Probably the most remarkable aspect of the desert campaigns is how the appalling heat, particularly when the tanks were closed down, had little effect on the efficiency of the tank crews.

The Enemy
Most Axis soldiers in North Africa were Italians, but, as far as the 1st Armoured Division was concerned the most important enemies were the mobile forces under General Rommel. The listing given below is a reasonable approximation for these troops in the desert, but not in Tunisia:

Armoured Group Africa, commander Field Marshal Rommel
    German Africa Corps (DAK) – Lt Gen Nehring
        15th Panzer Division – Lt Gen G v Vaerst
        21st Panzer Division – Maj Gen G v Bismarck
    90th Light Division – Maj Gen U Kleeman
    The 20th Italian Mobile Corps – Gen E Baldassare
        Ariete Armoured Division – Gen G de Stefanis
        Trieste Motorised Division – Gen Azzi.

Notes

1 The standard British tank radio set of the time was the Wireless Set No 19. This was, in its day, a very advanced system. It comprised three facilities in the one box: the 'A' set for communicating back to regiment, the 'B' set for inter-tank communications, and an intercom within the tank. The 'A' and 'B' sets gave voice communications ranges of 10 miles and 1,000 yards, respectively, using an eight foot rod aerial. The 'A' set could reach 15 miles with morse.

2 'Laager' is the term currently favoured by the Royal Armoured Corps, and it was used in Modern Formations. During the war 'leaguer' was used in the desert and 'harbour' in Europe, 'laager' seems a reasonable amalgam of these terms, and will be used in this study.

Chapter 6
Retreat to Gazala

The division, excluding 22nd Armoured Brigade, started to arrive at Suez during the second half of November 1941. The division reconnaissance regiment, 12th Lancers, and its artillery were immediately forwarded to the 8th Army and the 2nd Armoured Brigade commenced intensive training.

The situation in North Africa was that the Crusader battle was grinding to a halt, one based on mutual exhaustion, consequently it was natural for the British command to try to get reinforcements in action as soon as possible. However the situation improved when, on 7th December, Rommel decided to pull his forces back, initially to the Gazala position but later all the way back to Agedabia. On 18th December the division was ordered forward to join in the pursuit, but due to fuel shortage it was halted to the south-east of Tobruk where the bulk of the division spent a miserable Christmas.

However by 21st December the HQ and support group of the division had taken over from 7th Armoured Division, and the 22nd Armoured Brigade, which had been made up to nearly full strength and returned to the division, had replaced the 4th Armoured Brigade at Mechili. This brigade was immediately ordered to drive south-west in an attempt to cut off the axis forces in the manner of the Beda Fomm success, but failed due to lack of fuel.

By 28th December 22nd Guards Brigade was to the north of Agedabia and 22nd Armoured Brigade was around 25 miles to its south. *(See Sketch 3)* The Germans noticed this gap and struck the armoured brigade, driving it over 10 miles to the south and destroying 37 tanks for the loss of seven. Two days later the Germans repeated this success, knocking out 23 tanks for seven of their own. They then pulled back to El Agheila, and 22nd Armoured Brigade pulled back to refit, but left a composite squadron of 24 Honeys with 1st Support Group.

The 2nd Armoured Brigade concentrated 35 miles to the south west of Mersa Matruh, then set off on a 400 miles march on its tracks. It arrived at Saunna on 10th January and the 7th Armoured Division retired eastwards.

On 3rd January 1942 the division came under XIII Corps and Major-General Messervy[1] replaced Major-General Lumsden temporarily as the latter had been injured in an air attack. There was soon a re-shuffling of units. The organisation which the 2nd Armoured Brigade had trained with in England was one battery of the 11th (HAC) regiment RHA and one company of 9th Battalion RB attached to each of the armoured regiments, but now these supporting troops were withdrawn and, fairly soon, replaced by South African field and AT batteries. Unfortunately the South Africans, willing soldiers though they were, had no experience of working with tanks, fewer radios than did the British units they replaced and, as there was a dire shortage of fuel, there was no opportunity for training with the new organisation. At around this date the division received a company of 35 tank transporters. This unit was soon diverted to moving Valentines for Army Tank Brigades as infantry tanks were judged to be less mobile than cruisers.

The lack of opportunity for training was badly felt. The armoured regiments contained both Cruiser and Honey tanks, which initially were in homogenous squadrons. This organisation was changed to mixed squadrons with the SHQs in Honeys only to be changed back again. Also the regiments had hitherto used squadron nets for radio communications and this was changed to regimental nets. The logic being that in France, and England, the Colonel would never be able to see his entire regiment, but in the desert he would. These changes could not be trialled in exercises. This was all made that bit more difficult by the Honeys and Crusaders having different radios that used different frequencies.

The command situation was improved slightly by brigades and division HQs being issued with armoured command vehicles, ACV2s. These were, in effect, armoured lorries, fitted for radios and to be used as mobile offices. They were not always popular, being big and difficult to hide, but despite that they stayed in service with the division until it was disbanded. In France, in 1940, the division had used a mild steel prototype.

The artillery regiment and infantry battalion were formed into four battery-and-company 'Jock' columns to patrol forward and maintain a screen roughly in the El Agheila area. The withdrawal of the RHA batteries from the armoured regiments was naturally not welcomed by the armoured brigade which complained bitterly, but the new divisional commander, who had seen plenty of action in Operation Crusader and, no doubt, realised how inadequate a defence against tanks the 2-pdr was, believed that the AT defence must rest on 25-pdrs and he refused to change his orders.

The new organisation was to prove disastrous and is the likely origin of the intense and harmful antipathy between Generals Messervy and Lumsden. However hindsight is a wonderful thing and it can obscure an appreciation of the situation as it was at the time. There were two important facts facing General Messervy. One was the intelligence assessment that the Germans were exhausted and in no position to mount any real offensive. The other was his shortage of fuel. Taking these into account, harassing the Germans with Jock columns and keeping his tanks for counter-attacks must seem sensible.

The corps commander was certainly not expecting the Germans to attack, his view was that this was a quiet period while supplies were being built up for the next advance. His orders were to generally harass the enemy with Jock columns, and to be ready to fight a defensive action on the line Agebadia-El Haseiat. Unfortunately the only troops available for such a defence were little more than the armoured division, which was missing an armoured brigade, and the 200th Guards Brigade, which had only two battalions. He decided to man an advanced position running from Mersa

Brega to the Wadi Faregh. The 1st Support Group, which was effectively four Jock columns and an understrength artillery regiment, was on the left on this line, the Guards were on the right. The 2nd Armoured Brigade was at Antelat, the 22nd Armoured Brigade was at Tobruk refitting having left a composite squadron, known as 'Arthur Column' with the Support Group. The 12th Lancers were at Msus refitting. The division's main units were:

1st Armoured Division, Major-General Messervy
    12th Lancers
    2nd Armoured Brigade, Brigadier R Briggs
        The Queen's Bays
        9th Queen's Royal Lancers
        10th Royal Hussars
        One regiment RHA
        Two field regiments RA
        Two anti-tank regiments
        9th Battalion, The Rifle Brigade
    22nd Armoured Brigade, Brigadier J Scott-Cockburn
    1st Support Group, Brigadier CM Vallentin
        Composite Squadron, 3rd and 4th CLY
        One regiment RHA
        One field battery
        One anti-tank regiment RA
        Two light AA batteries
        1st Battalion, The Rifle Brigade.

Each of the three armoured regiments in 2nd Armoured Brigade had a strength of approximately 26 Cruisers and 18 Honeys, having lost several in the long drive forward.

The Germans struck at 8.00 am on 21st January 1942 and, in the face of superior force both the Support Group and the Guards Brigade fell back. The Support Group, after an engagement with 40 tanks, followed a route through soft sand and lost, through the day, 16 guns, but the soft going had the effect of slowing the Germans. By evening the Support Group had fallen back to the Agebadia-El Haseiat line with its left flank on El Haseiat. The Guards Brigade was slightly forward of this line.

General Messervy believed that the weak point in the British defence was the junction of the Support Group and the Guards Brigade, but next morning the Germans struck at Agebadia, by-passing the Guards, then proceeded on to Antelat. This had the effect of placing the Germans far behind the Support Group's right flank, and if they turned south then the Support Group would be cut off from its supplies at Msus, so the 2nd Armoured Brigade was ordered forward to Giof el Matar, a little over 20 miles behind El Haseiat. As the danger became more pronounced the brigade was ordered to concentrate 12 miles further north. It was also ordered to send a blocking force, based on an AT regiment, to the Agedabia-Antelat track, but failed to do this due to fuel shortage.

The brigade's 'B' echelons[2], one for each regiment and which included the workshops, were following the brigade at a respectful distance and halted for the night. They were attacked by a mixed Italian and German force which caused considerable damage before it withdrew. In this confused action the echelon personnel captured around 30 Italian troops, the division's first captures in Africa.

At some time during this period the 22nd Guards Brigade came under 1st Armoured Division and changed its title to 200th Guards Brigade. Its order of battle was:

200th Guards Brigade Group, Brigadier JCO Marriott
    B sqn, 11th Hussars
    3rd Bn Coldstream Guards
    2nd Bn Scots Guards
    Two field regiments RA
    One medium regiment RA
    Three AT batteries.

For a few days the brigade was joined by Arthur Column, then these tanks were handed over to 2nd Armoured Brigade and the CLY crews returned to Tobruk.

The question facing the division in the morning of 23rd January was how to avoid being cut off from Msus now that the Germans had reached Saunnu. The corps commander, General Godwin-Austen, radioed General Messervy that he must prevent the Germans reaching Msus so General Messervy sent the Queen's Bays to retake Saunnu, and the rest of the 2nd Armoured Brigade he sent to the Msus-Antelat track. The Guards and Support Group were to join them there.

When the Bays reached Saunnu they found that the Germans had left, they had gone to the south to block the Trig el Abd along which they assumed the British would retreat. The Germans had been significantly delayed by their own mines, which they had laid in the previous month. Not replacing the troops at Saunnu was a major mistake for the Germans. General Messervy ordered the 2nd Armoured Brigade to cover the western flank of the division as it retreated northwards. This resulted in the 9th Lancers coming into contact with German tanks around 10.0am. That stopped their progress north so the 10th Hussars passed them, but they were soon in action, presumably against the same German unit.

The brigade commander joined the Bays as they came up from Saunnu and got them on the Msus track. The other two regiments and the Support Group became involved in an extremely confusing action around Saunnu, the Hussars, in particular, closing to within 500 yards of the German tanks to be able to make effective use of their 2-pdrs and 37-mm guns, and so, despite extensive use of smoke having large numbers of tanks knocked out. Also the brigade suffered heavy casualties among their artillery, which the Panzer IV's seem to have handled easily. The Support Group escaped to the east, the two armoured regiments laagered up in the field.

Despite the confusion the bulk of the division, including the Guards, arrived at Msus next morning, 24th January. A brigade of the 11th Indian Division at Benghazi was moving south to form up on the western flank of the armoured division and the front seemed to be stabilising, even if the eastern flank was open. The Tank Delivery Squadron brought up 13 replacement tanks.

On 25th January the Germans attacked again, capturing Msus. The 1st Armoured Division retreated in the direction of Charruba where there was a supply dump. The German pursuit was petering out due to fuel shortage. However some German tanks did get close to the Advanced HQ. These were engaged by the Light AA Troop and one of the HQ defence troop tanks which knocked out a panzer IV and destroyed two AT guns by running over their trails forcing the remaining Germans to pull back. The Divisional HQ ACV2 broke down and had to be destroyed, the same fate seemed to have befallen the officers' mess wagon, but it was not competently smashed and a following unit brought it in.

The corps commander decided that retreat was the safer course and issued orders to that effect, ordering 1st Armoured Division to proceed to Mechili. Unfortunately the army commander, General Ritchie, did not agree and countermanded the retreat order.

The move to Charruba was fairly chaotic and carried out as fast as possible. It was ironically referred to as 'the Msus Stakes'. After it the armoured brigade was reconstituted as a composite regiment, the Lancers making up two squadrons, and the Bays and Hussars together making up the third squadron. This regiment slowly increased in size as some Honeys were sent forward from 22nd Armoured Brigade, and some tanks were recovered.

Both Generals Godwin-Austen and Messervy told the army commander that the tasks allotted to the division were impossible, but made no impression. General Messervy was not only to defend Charruba, but was to cover the eastern flank of the Indian brigade at Benghazi. He had 41 tanks and 40 field guns to do this with. General Ritchie believed that the Germans could be forced to halt if harassed by 'Jock' columns, but this was not the case.

On 27th January Rommel ordered a feint in the direction of Mechili then, next day, fell on Benghazi, but the armoured division could not help as it was manoeuvring in the Mechili direction.

After the fall of Benghazi General Ritchie accepted the inevitable and XIII Corps had returned to the Gazala line by 6th February. Because of their fuel situation, the Germans followed up only slowly, allowing the 2nd Armoured Brigade was re-equipped with tanks from 22nd Armoured Brigade which, in turn, was sent back to Egypt where it was partly re-equipped with Grants.

During the period of the retreat the 8th Army lost, according to the Official History, 1,390 personnel killed, wounded or missing, 42 tanks destroyed, 30 damaged or abandoned and 40 field guns. The overwhelming majority of these losses were incurred by 1st Armoured Division, but it should be noted that AFV casualties are always a little vague as many vehicles were recovered and returned to fighting units. At least 1st Armoured Division had not fallen apart as 2nd Armoured Division did the previous year when Rommel first struck, in remarkably similar circumstances.

In advancing to the west of Gazala the 8th Army had overreached itself, perhaps memories of Beda Fomm had distorted judgement. The result was that there were too few troops facing the Germans, and these troops were badly supplied and were lacking desert experience. General Messervy believed that troops needed three months intensive desert training before being fit for operations in North Africa. Rommel did not agree.

Naturally General Messervy had to produce a report to explain how his division was driven back so far and so fast. This report is of interest, it is in two parts, the first is a narrative of the division's operations and is neatly typed up. The second part is hand written, presumably by the general, and is generally in need of tidying up. No doubt the stresses of the Gazala battle prevented it being typed up. The whole paper may be read at Kew [3]. Some sections from it have been reproduced in appendix 2. These sections may be taken as being the general's comments on the performance of his division.

After the retreat, General Auchinleck observed to the Prime Minister that 'personnel in the Royal Armoured Corps are in some instances losing confidence in their equipment.'

Notes

1   Quite often this officer's name is spelt 'Masservy'. This is an error.

2   The echelons were responsible for the supply of the regiments. The 'A' echelons contained about half the supply vehicles of the regiments, their task was to provide their regiments with fuel and ammunition for one day's fighting. The 'B' echelons contained the remaining vehicles, their task was to collect supplies from dumps established by brigade and divisional transport companies, and bring them up to the 'A' echelons.
   The 'A' echelons, usually, had responsibility for the Regimental Aid Post and the regimental fitters. The 'B' echelon usually had responsibility for the regimental workshops

3   TNA CAB 106/662 Western Desert: report on operations 1942 Jan. 21 – Feb. 4 by Major-General FW Messervy, Commander

Chapter 7
The Battle of Gazala

After the retreat there was something of a lull while both sides recruited their strength. Two changes in particular affected the 1st Armoured Division. One was the issue of Grant tanks, the other was the organisation of brigade groups.

The Grant was the American tank with a 37-mm gun in the turret and a 75-mm gun in the hull. It was very popular being roomy and reliable, in fact it was dubbed ELH, 'Egypt's Last Hope'. Unfortunately Grants were tall, and the Germans tended to concentrate their fire on them.

The command of 1st Armoured Division reverted to General Lumsden, who had recovered from his wound, and General Messervy returned to the command of 7th Armoured Division. The antipathy between these two is well known and could possibly have been the result of Lumsden's criticism of Messervy's handling of the division in January and February.

General Ritchie had decided to fight a defensive battle and his two armoured divisions were combined as XXX Corps and located centrally behind the Gazala position expecting to be used for counter-attacks. *(See Sketch 4)*

When the Gazala battle started, on 26th May 1942, the British forces involved can be summarised as:

Eighth Army, commander Lieutenant General NM Ritchie
    5th Indian Division – Maj Gen HR Briggs
    XIII Corps – Lt Gen WHE Gott
        1st and 32nd Army Tank Brigades
        Three infantry divisions
    XXX Corps – Lt Gen CWM Norrie
        1st Armoured Division – Maj Gen H Lumsden
            2nd and 22nd Armoured Brigade Groups
            201st (previously 200th) Guards (Motor) Brigade

7th Armoured Division – Maj Gen FW Messervy
   4th Armoured Brigade Group
   7th Motor Brigade Group
   3rd Indian Motor Brigade Group
   29th Indian Infantry Brigade Group
   1st Free French Brigade Group

Although Brigade Groups are properly so called, the word 'Group' will be left off from now on.

General Auchinleck had observed that the standard of co-operation between the arms was poor so, in an attempt to improve this, he organised brigade groups. As has been seen it was already the practice to organise *ad-hoc* groupings like this but now they were to be permanent. The idea seemed to be an excellent one but experience was to show that it resulted in the brigades becoming more independent and less likely to function as parts of a division. In fact this battle was to show the British forces acting almost entirely as independent brigades, and the impression is that the existence of the divisional level of command served only to slow down the transmission of orders and cause confusion, at least among armoured forces.

The two armoured brigade groups of 1st Armoured Division were:

2nd Armoured Brigade, Brigadier R Briggs
   The Queen's Bays
   9th Queen's Royal Lancers
   10th Royal Hussars
   11th (HAC) Regiment, RHA
   76th AT regiment, RA
   1st Bn, RB

22nd Armoured Brigade, Brigadier J Scott-Cockburn
   3rd County of London Yeomanry
   4th County of London Yeomanry
   2nd Royal Gloucestershire Hussars
   107th RHA
   102nd AT regiment, RA
   50th Reconnaissance Regiment.

At this time a reconnaissance regiment was much the same as an infantry battalion with extra transport. The 50th battalion had previously been the 4th Northumberland Fusiliers. The 102nd AT regiment had been the Northumberland Hussars and the 107th RHA had been the South Notts. Hussars.

The procedure was to allocate each armoured regiment a field battery, a company of infantry and two troops of AT guns. Put together these three units were referred to as the 'regimental box'. This reorganisation was carried out in time for the battle but, unfortunately, there was no time to work out drills and tactics. This organisation was broken up and faded away during the Gazala battle and the subsequent retreat to Alamein.

The two armoured divisions together with their immediate reserves had a total of 573 tanks, comprising: 167 Grants, 149 Honeys and 257 Crusaders, each regiment had one squadron of Grants, and two of Crusaders/Honeys. The two Army Tank Brigades had a total of 276 Infantry tanks.

The British armoured forces were not well placed to meet the assault. This is believed to have been the result of lack of understanding down the chain of command. Essentially General Auchinleck believed the German assault would come in the north. He wanted the armoured brigades concentrated to the north of the Trig Capuzzo. General Ritchie was not totally convinced. He wanted to cover the possibility of the Germans coming round the south of the Line. To that end he moved 7th Armoured Division a little to the south, expecting the Corps Commander, Norrie, to concentrate the two armoured divisions once the main thrust of the German attack was identified. The operations of 7th Armoured Division were hampered by the locations of some of its brigades. These were scattered to the south and would be easily overrun by Rommel's troops unless armoured troops were rushed to their rescue, and this would inevitably happen before the armoured divisions had time to concentrate. The 201st Guards Brigade was posted in the 'Knightsbridge' box, a large defensive position about 15 miles south-west of Tobruk and 13 miles east of the Gazala minefields. 2nd Armoured Brigade was three miles to the east of Knightsbridge and 22nd Armoured Brigade was four miles to its south-west.

General Norrie's orders to his two armoured divisions were:

1st Armoured Division, two alternative tasks:
> *either*, to counter-attack enemy armoured formations directed on Tobruk by way of Acroma or El Adem after breaking through our minefields;
> *or*, to co-operate with the 7th Armoured Division against enemy armoured forces moving round Bir Hacheim.

7th Armoured Division:
> to defend Bir Hacheim to the last and to destroy any enemy forces moving round Bir Hacheim.

There were several factors that would prevent the British armour working in harmony. The human factor is commonly dwelt on and was probably the most significant. The corps and divisional commanders did not have much regard for the army commander, but they did for General Auchinleck. If Auchinleck said that the threat was in the north that is where it was, and they were reluctant to cover any supposed threat in the south. Secondly the corps commander, General Norrie, seems to have had little control over his divisional commanders, in fact it is tempting to wonder if, as already suggested, this extra level of command was just a nuisance. Finally General Lumsden thought Messervy to be incompetent and was very reluctant to see any of his troops coming under his command. Perhaps it would have been for the best if, at the first sign that the battle was starting, General Norrie had concentrated his armoured brigades and taken personal charge, as Rommel would have done.

Just before the battle started two General Routine Orders were issued. One was to the effect that nobody was to call Rommel a good general. The other was that no battle-worthy tank was to pick up the crew of a knocked out tank. The first of these orders was merely fatuous, the second, if enforced, would have been very detrimental to the morale of the tank crews. Fortunately few Colonels passed these orders on to the troops.

27th May 1942
The battle really began at 8.30 pm on the previous evening when Rommel instructed the Armoured Group Africa to start its move. This move went remarkably smoothly and by daybreak the 10,000 or so vehicles had rounded Bir Hacheim and were poised to surge north. Only one division was missing, the motorised infantry Trieste, which was still following earlier orders and working its way through the minefield to the north of Bir Hacheim.

Rommel probably flattered himself with the belief that he had achieved surprise, but he hadn't. His movements had been reported to 7th Armoured Division and the XXX Corps, but so strong was the effect of Auchinleck's prediction that the Germans would attack in the north that the Axis movements were taken to be solely attempts at deception. Perhaps the German feat of moving through the night baffled the British command. Either way the British response was disgracefully slow.

The huge force swung northwards and started overrunning scattered brigades. By 9.00 am German troops had progressed a further 10 miles north and captured the Advanced HQ, 7th Armoured Division, along with the divisional commander. Fortunately General Messervy, posing as a private soldier, managed to escape after only a few hours, but even so during this critical period the division's GOC was missing. The other German troops, the DAK, struck 4th Armoured Brigade and after a hard fight, destroyed it. However this action did force a delay on Rommel and he was critical of his commanders for accepting such a slogging match rather than covering the British with AT guns and out flanking them with tanks. This was what they finally did, bringing up three batteries of 88s.

Fortunately while all this was in train General Norrie ordered 1st Armoured Division to move to the south, then he set off in his staff car to HQ 7th Armoured Division where he was lucky not to be captured. He was, though, out of contact with his command for several hours. Perhaps Norrie's orders were not very insistent, or perhaps General Lumsden, the expert in armoured warfare, was like so many others convinced that any German move round Bir Hacheim would be a feint, but the reaction of the 1st Armoured Division was lethargic. The colonels of 2nd Armoured Brigade were called to an 'O' group at 9.45am and informed of the German advance. They could actually hear the fighting and had done so for over two hours. The brigade formed up and was ready to move south at 11.00am.

By this time the DAK had progressed north for 10 miles and hit 22nd Armoured Brigade, catching it totally by surprise. The brigade was positioned to face north. The southern-most regiment, the 2nd Royal Gloucestershire Hussars, was in reserve but was actually the first hit. Oddly the British tanks were ordered not to open fire because it was thought that the German tanks were the survivors of 4th Armoured Brigade, a mistake that was soon rectified. In an action that only lasted 20 minutes the regiment lost about 30 tanks, the Grant squadron being reduced to one tank. The survivors withdrew to the Knightsbridge box. The other two regiments of the brigade initially were ordered to fall in line with 2RGH, but then were pulled back to the north-east to join 2nd Armoured Brigade. They were pursued by the Germans and, because of the slow cross-country speed of the Grants, decided to stand and fight. The battle lasted 30 minutes, around 13 of the brigade's tanks were knocked out and the survivors continued their retreat which now placed them to the rear of the 2nd Armoured Brigade which was yet to move, but the Germans lost some tanks and their progress was checked if only for a short time by the newly-issued 6-pdrs of the AT batteries.

The Germans now, under the impression that the British armour was defeated, surged on northwards to try to cut the

Trig Capuzzo. General Lumsden's obvious task was to organise a counter-attack, his problem was to get his two armoured brigades to co-operate when one of them had been badly mauled, and he could not have been sure of the location of the enemy when 2nd Armoured Brigade started south. The brigade moved *en bloc* in the usual arrowhead formation, with the Hussars taking point, the Lancers on the right and the Bays to the left. It was soon in action. The Hussars had an inconclusive long range action and drove some German tanks off, but the Bays came under fire from the west and quickly had the entire right hand troop knocked out, the troop leader was among the dead. As it became plain that the Germans were present in force the brigade commander ordered 'Action Right', the Bays prepared to engage to the west, the Hussars swung round to the left of the Bays and the Lancers to their right. The brigade must have been a magnificent sight.

This was around 2.15pm, and a quarter of an hour later the two CLY regiments of 22nd Armoured Brigade, 2RGH now being *hors de combat*, came up on the right of 2nd Armoured Brigade, that is from the north. Also the Germans were attacked from the west by 44RTR which was a part of 1st Army Tank Brigade. This regiment attacked gallantly and lost 18 Matilda II's. The Germans were in a potentially disastrous position.

At this point General Lumsden arrived and ordered the brigade to attack the Germans who turned out to be a battalion of lorried infantry. The Germans deployed their AT guns, but the Bays and the Lancers[1] were too fast for them, and they would not have expected the 75-mm HE fire of the Grants. The regiments sent their Grants forward to engage initially at 3,000 yards, but soon they advanced to half that range. As the fire was seen to be effective the Crusader squadrons were sent charging in at different angles and over 200 German soldiers surrendered which effectively destroyed one German battalion. Also 15 AT guns were knocked out. The Rifle Brigade troops were on hand to round up the prisoners.

A sandstorm blew up as 4.00 which effectively ended the fighting and, it is reasonable to say, saved the Germans. It was 5.30pm before the brigade had reformed and was ready to advance westwards, but, before it could start, it was ordered back to its previous position close to Knightsbridge. After the brigade had returned there the Bays lost a further Grant which, as the regimental history recounts, caught fire when its crew were brewing tea inside it.

At the end of the day the British situation must have looked a little bleak, the 7th Armoured Division was *hors de combat*, and 22nd Armoured Brigade had been badly mauled, but the Germans' situation was much worse, so the 1st Armoured Division could feel satisfied with its day.

28th May

The day was to be something of an anticlimax following the high drama of the 27th. The vulnerability of the Germans was not recognised by General Lumsden whose main priority seems to have been the security of Knightsbridge. 22nd Armoured Brigade spent the day to its east and 2nd Armoured Brigade spent the greater part of the day to its south.

2nd Armoured Brigade moved off at first light and after about two miles came into contact with some German AT guns. 10th Hussars, which was again point, started to suffer casualties and 9th Lancers came up on its left to assist. However the tank guns, including those of the Grants, could not subdue the fire of the AT guns so an assault was decided upon. The 11th RHA and the two regiments brought down a heavy fire, the RHA firing first HE then smoke, then one squadron of Hussars Crusaders charged. They did this in two waves. The first wave, of ten tanks, charged through the German position, wheeled to the right and returned to the regimental position. The second wave, of five tanks and including the Squadron Leader, stayed on the objective to destroy the guns. This tactic worked perfectly and 35 Germans surrendered to be brought back riding on the tanks, seven guns and one half-track were destroyed. One tank was lost, it was commanded by a troop leader. It was in the first wave and wheeled left instead of right. A tank by itself was so often an easy target and the wreck was later found about a mile away.

This minor British success was good for morale, but it may have contributed to a disaster later in the day.

The brigade stayed watching to the south until early afternoon when General Lumsden came to the brigade and ordered it to the west, leaving the Bays where they were. After around three hours the Bays were ordered to rejoin the brigade. Then the brigade was ordered to attack to the west, into the setting sun.

Opposition was not heavy though the Germans were thought to have lost five tanks, but the advance had started too late to produce significant results. It was marred by a disaster to the left hand squadron, a Crusader squadron of 10th Hussars. This squadron forged ahead in among the axis AT guns alone and unsupported and was destroyed, practically the entire squadron was taken prisoner. At the end of the day the 2nd Armoured Brigade returned to the positions it held at its start.

The actions of 1st Armoured Division were disappointing and it is difficult to understand the lack of drive. It seems that General Lumsden's chief concern was to keep his armoured brigades out of action in case they came under 7th Armoured Division's control. Neither division used its infantry in co-operation with its tanks.

29th May
At first light 2nd Armoured Brigade moved to the south and quickly had a short and successful action against some German infantry and 22nd Armoured Brigade, in effect the two CLY regiments, took up a position to the south-west of Knightsbridge. Then the regiments started making breakfast.

This quiet did not last long and soon a large number of German tanks was seen to the west, estimated from 80 to

100. The 2nd Armoured Brigade formed up into an arrowhead, Bays leading, the Lancers to the left and Hussars to the right and surged off to the west to attack the Germans. They drove through the CLY position, but 22nd Armoured Brigade was not called on to co-operate in the attack. Unfortunately the attack ran into the area where Rommel was concentrating his armour and soon the brigade had 15th Panzer Division to its west, 21st Panzer to its north and the Ariete to its south. The brigade halted and the battle became a slogging match. The battle started at 11.00 am, and after an hour the CLY were called forward and formed up on the flanks . The Germans mounted a succession of attacks and 10th Hussars, on the right, lost all their tanks. The other regiments suffered much less.

The fighting was halted first by a sandstorm then by the onset of night. The 2nd Armoured Brigade laagered up *in situ* with the CLY occupying the gap between 2nd Armoured Brigade and Knightsbridge.

The 1st Armoured Division could claim that it had maintained the security of Knightsbridge, which was its main objective, but really this action had been an undeniable defeat for the British. It was not obvious at the time as the Germans were pulling back to the 'Cauldron', but with hindsight it can be seen as the decisive point of the Gazala battle.

The 'Cauldron' was an easily defensible area backing on to the Gazala Line, bounded to the north by Sidra Ridge and to the east by Aslagh Ridge. Its greatest width, east-west, was about 10 miles. To occupy this area the Germans had to destroy an infantry box held by the 150th Brigade. The existence of this box came as a surprise to Rommel who had no choice but to assault it. The battle was desperate, lasting two days. His forces became short of everything, specially water, and he was within a few hours of surrendering his forces when the defence started to crack. Unfortunately the British, who also had suffered badly in the first phase of the battle, did not realise what a desperate situation Rommel was in.

The northern face of the Cauldron, Sidra Ridge, was occupied by the 21st Panzer Division, and Aslag Ridge by the Ariete. The 90th Light faced the 150th Brigade and 15th Panzer Division was in reserve, generally facing south.

30th May
At first light the Germans were seen to be retreating, and this was confirmed by midday by aerial reconnaissance. The 9th Lancers were sent to attack the German rearguard, but made no impression mostly because the last mile and a half were across open desert. They were sent back to try again at 3.30 pm and were given two troops from the 2nd RGH to help but still failed. The smoke screen that had been fired was totally ineffective and the Germans were in hull-down positions on a slight ridge. After this action the 9th Lancers were withdrawn from the fighting. The 22nd Armoured Brigade spent the day watching or skirmishing to the south of Knightsbridge.

As far as British armour was concerned the day was one of wasted opportunities, in fact it was the start of a general lull in operations which lasted until 5th June. The 150th Brigade battle was just getting started and Rommel's troops were vulnerable to a determined assault, but the chance was let slip as it was on the next day as well. General Lumsden, reluctant to see his armour shot to pieces, wanted a night attack to be made by infantry to neutralise the Axis AT guns and open a way for his tanks. This plan was too ambitious to put into practice at such short notice. Perhaps the reactions of the British armour would have been faster if the HQs of the 8th Army and XXX Corps were not forty miles away to the east.

31st May
There was no action on this day. The 9th Lancers were ordered to hand over their few remaining tanks to the Bays and the crews were sent to the rear for re-equipping. This left

2nd Armoured Brigade as effectively only the Bays. The 22nd Armoured Brigade was reorganised as one composite regiment.

1st/3rd June

On these days the 1st Armoured Division did very little but watch German armour probing to the north of the Cauldron. The 150th Brigade, with most of 1st Army Tank Brigade, surrendered and Rommel could turn his attention to reducing Bir Hacheim. The initiative was slipping away from the British, but tanks were being repaired and sent back to the armoured brigades.

4th June

By this date Rommel had 130 serviceable tanks, less than half the number he started the battle with. The British had about 400. Despite this superiority there was a lack of decisiveness in the command structure. There was an obvious need to regain the initiative and assault the Cauldron. This was to be Operation Aberdeen, and it turned out to be one of the most mismanaged and disastrous operations undertaken by the British army. 1st Armoured Division was not directly involved, but its two armoured brigades were, so a brief account of the operation will be given.

Inevitably the operation would involve troops from both corps, from XIII Corps in the north and XXX Corps in the east. It would have been most sensible to have had one commander for the whole operation and General Gott was asked to do this but would not accept. So General Ritchie decided to retain overall command himself with the fighting being controlled by either the armoured division commander, General Messervy, or the infantry commander, General Briggs, depending on whether the fighting was in the initial, infantry, stage, or the later, armoured, stage. The XXX Corps commander, General Norrie, seems to have been left out of the chain of command.

While the British were sorting themselves out, so were the Germans. They not only repaired tanks but cleared lanes through the minefield to the south and east of the Cauldron for the use of counter-attacking troops.

The bulk of the fighting on the XXX Corps front was to be done by the 22nd Armoured Brigade which had 156 tanks, a mixture of the three types. In particular the 2nd RGH had been given the tanks of the 4th Hussars, something that is difficult to understand. The regiment had been transferred from 1st Armoured Division to the 7th to replace the 4th Armoured Brigade which had been withdrawn due to heavy casualties, a move no doubt bitterly contested by General Lumsden. The essence of the British plan was an Indian infantry brigade assault on the Aslagh Ridge, it would be carried out at night and would be supported by the Valentines of 4RTR. Following this, at dawn, the 22nd Armoured Brigade would burst through into the centre of the Cauldron, destroying any Axis armour it met, and finish up at point B104 just to the south of Sidra Ridge. It would be followed by another Indian infantry brigade which would dig in to consolidate the ground taken by the armour. A secondary assault was to be mounted by XIII Corps on Sidra Ridge. It was to be carried out by 32nd Army Tank Brigade supported by an infantry battalion, its left flank being covered by the depleted 4th Armoured Brigade. This action was not coordinated with that of XXX Corps.

5th June

The XIII Corps operation started in the early morning. The artillery barrage commenced at 2:50 am and by dawn the leading infantry were on the ridge. Unfortunately the weight of the artillery preparation had fallen on empty desert, the Italian defenders had decoyed the British into thinking their defences were half a mile in front of their real locations. The real fighting started at dawn and the infantry suffered greatly but it was judged that they had carried out their task and the 22nd Armoured Brigade was sent through.

The brigade, in its usual arrowhead formation with 2nd RGH taking point, moved as fast as visibility allowed and covered around two miles, then ran into the German and Italian artillery. The only reason they were not annihilated was that the shells raised so much dust that the gunners could not see their targets. It also made it harder for the tanks to fire back. All this caused them to swing north but here they ran into the AT guns of the 21st Panzer Division and pulled back behind some infantry who were digging in. The brigade had lost 60 tanks out of its initial strength of 156.

The withdrawal of the armour left the infantry vulnerable and the German and Italian armour counter-attacked causing devastation. The armoured brigade, whose orders included the statement, '*In the case of armoured action infantry are self-protecting. They will not hamper the movement of 22nd Armoured Brigade*', refused to help the infantry, which was finally forced to retreat, its 2-pdr AT guns, not dug in, being easily knocked out. The armour then pulled back with it. The assault here had failed.

Afterwards one of the two infantry brigade commanders commented that in the desert a brigade needed 48 hours to set up a tank proof position, that is one able to survive without armoured support, but according to its orders this was of no concern to the armoured brigade.

The attack of the 32nd Army Tank Brigade on Sidra Ridge was a disaster. 70 infantry tanks advanced in broad daylight, with minimal artillery support, against the 21st Panzer Division, and ran into a minefield. They lost 50 tanks and achieved nothing.

By mid afternoon the British attack had ground to a halt. There had been a chance to throw in the 2nd Armoured Brigade which had been 20 miles away to the north. It was brought up and placed under 7th Armoured Division, but it received from it a number of contradictory orders and was not used. As it only had one regiment of tanks it would probably not have achieved much.

At 5.00pm Rommel ordered a general counter-attack. The 21st Panzer Division attacked to the north, passing the wreckage of 32nd Tank Brigade. It then swung to the east, then to the south to hit the flank of 22nd Armoured Brigade and the two infantry brigades on the Aslagh Ridge.

The Ariete in the middle attacked eastwards towards Aslagh Ridge, pinning down the infantry brigades there. Elements of the 15th Panzer Division, under the direct command of Rommel, passed through the minefield to the south of the ridge and at this point the Germans were joined by a battlegroup withdrawn from the Bir Hacheim fighting. They overran unit after unit and also overran the HQ of the 7th Armoured Division. This was one of the few double envelopments that modern warfare has seen.

The defence against such an envelopment should be troops and artillery positioned to fight, as it were, sideways to prevent the line being rolled up, and a reserve. As it was all the artillery was close to the ridge and facing the Cauldron, and the 2nd Armoured Brigade was left without orders. The nearest significant unit, the 201st Guards Brigade, was hit by the Luftwaffe and immobilised. The Germans mopped up the remaining infantry units of the Aslagh Ridge next day.

Around half of the 22nd Armoured Brigade escaped, again giving no assistance to the infantry. It is just possible that, with some Rommel-type leadership, it could have joined the 2nd Armoured Brigade and perhaps some of the 201st Guards Brigade troops and counter-attacked to allow the escape of some of the surrounded units, but the reality is that a rout takes a long time to halt. And there is no doubt that it was a rout. It could be that desert fighting results in a frame of mind that prefers movement to fighting for every foot of ground, and certainly some units fell back too quickly. Some fought very well. When the Ariete tanks assaulted Aslagh Ridge, one group of four 25-pdrs stayed in action to the end, the last gunner running from one gun to another until he, in his turn, was killed.

In many ways the abandonment of the Indian infantry brigades, no matter how it could have been justified, marked a distinct turning point in the reputation of British armour. Before Operation Aberdeen the British armour had basked in the afterglow of Wavell's campaign, and Operation Crusader, despite its many setbacks, had been a success. But after Operation Aberdeen, the reputation of the armour sank from one low point to the next until Montgomery changed everything at Alam Halfa.

The rock that armour's reputation foundered on was co-operation with infantry. Previously that co-operation had been left to the infantry tanks, that was no longer possible after Operation Aberdeen, but unfortunately the whole ethos of Cruiser Tank Warfare made such co-operation nearly impossible. The blame for this must ultimately be laid at the door of those who wrote the manuals and designed the tanks for the armoured divisions.

The end of the Cauldron fighting was followed by the fall of Bir Hacheim on 9th June. After that it was plain that the initiative was in Rommel's hands. Unfortunately the British command was still optimistic.

In the few days available before Rommel resumed the offensive it would have been impossible to realign the British forces to cope with the new situation. Ideally the Gazala Line would have been evacuated, the troops and such mines and wire as were available sent to defend Tobruk. Tobruk was Rommel's obvious target. The armour should have been concentrated into one division, and some infantry boxes, such as Knightsbridge, retained and strengthened to act as pivots for the coming tank battles when Rommel tried to surround Tobruk. Instead, following the Cauldron disaster the armoured brigades were pulled back to the north of, and close to, Knightsbridge. 1st Armoured Division took command of 22nd Armoured Brigade and 32nd Army Tank Brigade, and 7th Armoured Division had 2nd and 4th Armoured Brigades.

Although tank strengths fluctuated wildly, at this time they were given as:

1st Armoured Division
    22nd Armoured Bde, 27 Grants, 34 Crusaders, 5 Stuarts
    32nd Army Tank Brigade, 63 Infantry tanks.

7th Armoured Division
    2nd Armoured Brigade, 17 Grants, 25 Crusaders, 3 Stuarts
    4th Armoured Brigade, 39 Grants and 56 Stuarts
    7th Motor Brigade, 16 Stuarts.

Even despite the recent disasters the British command was reasonably optimistic. Following the destruction of Bir Hacheim the southern wing of the Gazala Line now bent back east to Knightsbridge and El Adem. This re-deployment was carried out under the control of XIII Corps and General Gott. The result of this should have been a strong position which Rommel could not by-pass, and the British armour should have been able, even after everything, to stand against Rommel's. The Germans had 200 tanks, but this total included 85 second class tanks, either Italian or Panzer II's, but of course it is always difficult to know exactly how well aware of the German situation the British were. The result of the coming action should not have been a foregone conclusion.

6th June

The retreat from the Cauldron did not signal the end of that phase of the battle. The 22nd Armoured Brigade pulled back from the infantry and spent the night with the tanks to the south of Knightsbridge and the artillery to its west. At dawn the tanks were rushed to the east when 4th Armoured Brigade was under attack and needed assistance. This resulted in a long-range and inconclusive action during which, unfortunately, the Colonel of the 2nd RGH was killed.

While the tanks were occupied to the east, the brigade's artillery, the South Notts Hussars, was attacked by German tanks and was running short of ammunition. An attempt was made to send a convoy of 15 ammunition lorries, escorted by a troop of Crusaders from 3rd CLY, the two miles from

Knightsbridge to the guns. This convoy came under heavy fire and the tanks and 11 lorries were knocked out. The four lorries that got through were not enough to allow resistance to be maintained until the tanks could return and the regiment was overrun, fighting to the end in the finest tradition of the Royal Regiment. The 107th RHA (South Notts Hussars) then ceased to exist. In all, Operation Aberdeen saw the destruction of five artillery regiments, losses every bit as important as those among tanks.

Next day the 2nd RGH handed over their two remaining Grants to 3rd CLY. They never again fought as a complete regiment.

There followed a short lull in operations before the commencement of the third phase.

11th June
Final phase of the Gazala battle started in mid afternoon. Rommel's first move seems to have been something of a gambit to see which way the British would jump. He did not keep the DAK together, but left 21st Panzer Division in Sidra Ridge, and sent 15th Panzer Division to the north-east, from Bir Hacheim, towards El Adem. This division was supported on its left by the Trieste Motorised Division. On its right went the 90th Light Division. Presumably this division, now down to 1,000 men, was to establish itself to the east of Tobruk. The British were very sensitive about this area because of the supply dump at Belhammed.

The route of the 15th Panzer Division and the associated units was right between the 4th Armoured Brigade and the 7th Motorised Brigade and other 7th Armoured Division units. The armoured brigade started south from Knightsbridge but halted at Naduret el Ghesceuasc which, if not high ground, is slightly higher than the surrounding desert. The 15th Panzer Division had also halted and the two forces spent the night within extreme range of each other.

12th June
In the morning General Norrie ordered 2nd Armoured Brigade to join the 4th. These two brigades should have been able to strike a major blow against 15th Panzer Division, while 22nd Armoured Brigade held 21st Panzer Division and the Ariete in check. The 32nd Army Tank Brigade could be called on to help, but its main function was to prevent the northern sector of the Gazala line being outflanked. As can be seen, with the corps manoeuvring as brigade groups, the divisional organisation starts to look unsure and the capacity for misunderstanding grows.

This plan was sensible and realistic but failed utterly because the two brigade commanders would not accept General Messervy's plan. This was for 2nd Armoured Brigade, in the east, to pin down the 15th Panzer Division while 4th Armoured Brigade swung round to the west, linked up with 7th Motor Brigade, and then attacked the Germans from the flank and rear.

This plan, in its turn, was a good one, but it seems that 4th Armoured Brigade was reluctant to leave the high ground of Naduret el Ghesceuasc, and 2nd Armoured Brigade, though nominally a part of 7th Armoured Division, did not want to get involved in serious action away from 1st Armoured Division. The two brigades remained stationary. General Messervy, having failed to get his orders accepted, drove off to see General Norrie, ran into a German reconnaissance unit and spent the rest of the day hiding in a well.

The situation with the British armoured brigades was bad enough but their radio procedure made it worse and, via his radio intercept service, Rommel was soon aware of the hold-up in the British chain of command and he set out to exploit it.

Up to midday the armoured brigades and 15th Panzer were stationary, in long range contact, the superior armament of the Grants deterring the Germans. Then two things happened. General Norrie, realising that General Messservy was missing, put General Lumsden in command of all three armoured brigades. General Lumsden ordered 22nd Armoured Brigade south to join the other two. Rommel ordered the 21st Panzer Division to drive to the east with all speed, which it could do now that 22nd Armoured Brigade was no longer watching it, and engage the tanks facing the 15th Panzer Division.

The Germans were faster, probably because both Rommel and Nehring were driving them as hard as they could. The result was that the armoured brigades were hit on the south and the east, and some of the 21st Panzer Division started to lap round to the north. Not surprisingly casualties were heavy among British tanks. The Grant, with its main armament in the hull, could not take up a hull down firing position and, being on slightly higher ground, would have risen above any heat haze, and been an easy target. The DAK had recently received some Panzer III's with the longer barrelled 50-mm guns which, having a higher muzzle velocity, could penetrate the frontal armour of the Grants.

The situation of the 2nd and 4th Armoured Brigades was desperate, but they received a little respite when 22nd Armoured Brigade joined the fray. This gave 4th Armoured Brigade a chance to pull back, which it did with such vigour that it reached the Tobruk by-pass road, but with only 15 tanks. To try to use their Grants most effectively the two CLY regiments pooled their Grants to create two Grant units, what the regimental history terms 'task forces', each task force being in effect two troops. However this organisation seems to have offered no real advantage.

The 2nd and 22nd Armoured Brigades, fighting all the way, fell back to the east and north-east of Knightsbridge. This box was judged to be untenable without the support of strong British armour, and it was evacuated on the night of 13th/14th. The Gazala Line was then in danger of being cut off, so it was decided that it should be evacuated. To cover this operation the 2nd South African Division was ordered to hold the line of the minefield running from the coast south to

Acroma. This division was to be supported by 1st Armoured Division which took up a position between Acroma and the Commonwealth Keep, about ten miles to its west, in front of the minefield. In the region of five miles to the south of the Commonwealth Keep was a series of three boxes, running west to east, William's Post, Best Post and Point 187. The Germans attacked these posts early on 14th June.

The 1st Armoured Division did not have liaison officers at these posts, or any others, and may well have missed several opportunities of hitting the Germans in their flanks, even though 32nd Army Tank Brigade could not drive as fast as the Cruiser-based armoured brigades. The 2nd and 22nd Armoured Brigades were ordered to defend Acroma, regardless of cost, till dark. They succeeded in doing this, but 2nd Armoured Brigade was down to two Grants and eight Crusaders. At 8.30pm a general retreat was ordered which effectively signalled the surrender of Tobruk. 32nd Army Tank Brigade was last to leave, being for a short time, the rearguard of the entire army. It took up a position within the Tobruk perimeter, and was lost to 1st Armoured Division.

Note

1   Both the Bays and the 9th Lancers, in their regimental histories, claim sole credit for this engagement.

Chapter 8
The Retreat to Alamein

General Gott, commanding XIII Corps which had taken 1st Armoured Division under command on 12th June, ordered it to withdraw at 10.0 pm 14th June. It pulled back leaving two squadrons of the 9th Lancers with orders to join the 4th Armoured Brigade. On 15th June the Bays handed over their seven remaining tanks the 3rd CLY. The 201st Guards (motor) Brigade and 32nd Army Tank Brigade took up a position within the Tobruk perimeter from which very few personnel escaped.

The 9th Lancers had been withdrawn from the fighting after suffering heavy casualties at the Cauldron. It was re-equipped with all remaining available tanks before the Tank Delivery Regiment left for Egypt. It then had enough tanks for two squadrons: 12 Grants, 19 Crusaders and 3 Honeys. These two squadrons joined 4th Armoured Brigade on 17th June in time to take up a position at Sidi Rezegh on a slight ridge facing westwards. The brigade was widely scattered and the Lancer squadrons were the only tanks in the immediate vicinity, but they were well backed up by artillery and AT guns.

That must have seemed fortunate because they were soon attacked by what looked like a panzer division passing to the south of the Tobruk perimeter. Much to the Lancers' consternation the gunners limbered up and left, leaving the two squadrons alone. They stayed and fought but ultimately they were attacked by two panzer divisions, losing tanks not only to the Germans tanks but also to their AT guns which, following usual German tactics, were skilfully pushed forward. Had the British artillery stayed in the field the Germans could not have done that. In the end the surviving tanks retreated after firing smoke. The other regiments of 4th Armoured Brigade also took heavy casualties, this destroyed the last hope of putting in a serious counter-attack to save Tobruk.

When the 9th Lancer squadrons returned to 1st Armoured Division they had nine Grants, all damaged, only one of which could be repaired locally. The crews had to go back to Egypt for re-equipping.

The 8th Army pulled back to the Mersa Matruh position. That position and roughly 10 miles south of it were occupied by X Corps. South of that was XIII Corps, and XXX Corps was to collect and organise an armoured striking force, but this would be a long job.

Both armoured divisions came under XIII Corps, but 7th Armoured Division handed over all its tanks to the 1st, and maintained a motorised infantry screen in front of the main position. The 1st Armoured Division then had 155 tanks. Further to this the army possessed 19 Infantry tanks, giving a total of 174 tanks, significantly more than Rommel had and generally of better quality. This was the situation on 25th June when General Auchinleck took command of 8th Army and decided to conduct a fighting retreat to the Alamein position which at that time was only a mark on a map. *(See Sketch 5)*

The 1st Armoured Division's order of battle was:

Commander, Major-General H Lumsden
    4th Armoured Brigade, Brigadier AF Fisher
        9th Lancers (one squadron)
        1st RTR
        6th RTR
        8th RTR
    22nd Armoured Brigade, Brigadier J Scott-Cockburn
        3rd CLY
        4th CLY
   7th Motor Brigade
   3rd Indian Motor Brigade

The 2nd Armoured Brigade had been withdrawn from the active division to act as a unit for re-equipping and forwarding formations to the active armoured brigades. The tanks being issued had been taken from 8th Armoured Brigade which was a part of 10th Armoured Division that had just arrived from Syria. The now tankless 8th Armoured Brigade returned to the delta.

On 27th June the Germans attacked. The 15th Panzer Division was halted by 4th Armoured Brigade and 7th Motor Brigade, then these two brigades fell back slowly. To the north of 1st Armoured Division was with the New Zealand Division which was posted on the southern of two escarpments. Some panzers and other troops advanced to the north of this escarpment and were enveloping the New Zealanders from the east so, amid a confusion of orders, they retreated eastwards. The 1st Armoured Division had initially been called on to assist the New Zealanders, but when they left the armoured division had to head south east to a fuel dump at Bir Khalda. It arrived mid-morning 28th June. The 22nd Armoured Brigade took up a position to cover the coast road between Fuka and Daba, 4th Armoured Brigade was to its south. First RTR, to the west, became separated from the rest of the brigade and was by-passed by the leading German tanks. It was fortunate to be able to withdraw without casualties.

While this was happening the Queen's Bays, comprising two Honey and one Grant squadrons, with a squadron of 9th Lancers under command, having been re-equipped in 2nd Armoured Brigade, drove forward to 1st Armoured Division, no doubt adding to the general confusion. They bumbled around in the desert and lost two tanks in a long range engagement, and seven of the Lancers' nine Crusaders broke down. They passed the night in the desert and next day joined 22nd Armoured Brigade ten miles south of Fuka. The difficulties experienced by the Bays illustrate the problems caused in the open and featureless terrain by poor radio communications. Almost immediately the two Honey squadrons were sent north to co-operate with 12th Lancers in the Fuka area. They achieved little and returned to the regiment next day when they were joined by a battery of 25-

pdrs and a company of infantry, given the code name of 'Draffcol', after Colonel Draffen, and sent off in an independent role as a glorified Jock Column. Draffcol spent two days in what may be termed enemy territory, achieved little and was recalled. The surviving Honeys formed a composite squadron with some 4th Hussars tanks coming directly under the brigade's command, regimental HQ being withdrawn.

While this was happening the Grant squadron of the Bays was attached to 4th CLY and, on 30th June, took part in a very successful action against a column of, apparently, the Ariete. 4th CLY was fully equipped having just taken over the Grants and Honeys of the Royal Scots Greys. The tankless Greys were sent to the rear. This procedure of swapping tanks and not regiments is a little difficult to understand. 3rd CLY, having lost a large number of tanks, was temporarily broken up, with a Crusader squadron going to 4th Hussars and the Grants being retained as brigade protection troop.

As the 8th Army settled into to the Alamein position, the XXX Corps held the northern end of the line, mostly a perimeter round El Alamein. The XIII Corps was a string of widely separated units leading off southwards. The two armoured divisions, the 7th with no tanks, were withdrawn from XIII Corps to army reserve.

After a short lull, Rommel decided to attack again. He knew his troops were at their last gasp but he also knew that if the British were given any time to organise their defences he would never break through to the delta. He planned to burst through the British line just to the south of El Alamein, following which an Italian infantry division would attack that position from the east while the rest of the attacking force turned south to roll up the British line. However he did not take the time for a thorough reconnaissance and this was one occasion when he should have done so. On the southern shoulder of the proposed breakthrough at Deir el Shein was the 18th Indian brigade which he did not know about. The operation did not go well for the axis troops. The 90th Light

Division and DAK got lost overnight, then the Germans were held up by the Indian brigade. These delays gave 1st Armoured Division the opportunity to replenish and concentrate, the two armoured brigades being roughly five miles to the east of Deir el Shein and south of Ruweisat Ridge, but the 4th Armoured Brigade was bogged in soft sand.

The 18th Indian Brigade was well able to mount a formidable resistance. It consisted of three battalions each of which had three 2-pdrs and attached to it was the AT company of the Buffs with 16 6-pdrs. Unfortunately these guns had been issued only three days previously and the crews had had no training with them when this company arrived on 1st July. The brigade also received 23 25-pdrs and 12 2-pdrs, these being elements of three field regiments. They arrived on 30th June and the following night. Eight Matildas, manned by scratch crews, were attached to the brigade. There was a little wire and a partial minefield, but there had been far too little time to dig the guns in, the 48 hour rule mentioned earlier was proving to be a good one.

The German attack started at 8.00 am, then a dust storm blew up reducing visibility to 100 yards. The brigade sent a non-urgent call to XXX Corps at 11.00 am, but communications were so bad that the corps did not receive it till 5.00 pm. However the corps had been informed by a liaison officer of the situation at 1.20 pm. 1st Armoured Division, now a part of that corps, was ordered to go to the assistance of the brigade.

At 2.00 pm a German attack, led by 12 tanks, was through the wire and mines. It was driven back by the eight Matildas, but it had caused heavy casualties among the AT guns and 25-pdrs. During the lull following this attack the 1st Armoured Division was informed by one of its reconnaissance units that all was quiet at Deir el Shein and all urgency, it seems, was lost. The Germans attacked again at 4.0 pm, this time they were more successful. The Matildas were all knocked out and the surviving guns ran out of ammunition. As the position was being abandoned the only regiment left in 22nd Armoured Brigade, the 4th CLY with a squadron from the Bays arrived, it was not able to alter the outcome of the battle but it did have a successful fight with some German tanks, driving them off to the west. In this action the colonel of 4th CLY, Colonel Arkwright, was killed by shellfire while sitting on the back of a tank discussing the battle with the brigadier.

This essentially concluded the day's fighting, one of the results of which was that there were many who would say that 1st Armoured Division had let the Indian brigade down. The destruction of this brigade was disaster enough to warrant a Court of Enquiry, the papers of which may be read at Kew [1]. General Lumsden's statement is given in Appendix 3.

The court, in conclusion, made two criticisms:

> Due to inexperience the brigade staff failed to
>   communicate their situation to higher formations.
> The troops had no infantry AT weapons.

The second point is difficult to understand. There was no shortage of AT guns and there were some mines, but meaningful personal AT weapons at that time did not exist. The Boys rifle was obsolete and had been withdrawn and the PIAT was not yet issued. The court specifically mentioned Sticky Bombs, but these had never been issued in the Middle East.

It is debateable to what extent the assault of Deir el Shein was necessary to the Germans. It was carried out by the 21st Panzer Division and the assault and the immediate fighting with 22nd Armoured Brigade cost the division 18 tanks, this dramatically reduced the offensive capability of the DAK, but much worse than this was the loss of time. In the morning of 1st July the 1st Armoured Division was scattered and in disarray, if Rommel's tanks could have got in among the division then it is not fanciful to believe that the entire division could have been destroyed and the way to Egypt laid open. Despite this the stand and destruction of 18th Indian Infantry Brigade has been largely forgotten. It is worth noting that no British armoured division could have assaulted an infantry position as the 21st Panzer Division in this action.

On 2nd July it seemed that the German attacks had been held and Auchinleck wanted an immediate counter-attack. 1st Armoured Division was transferred back to XIII Corps with orders to attack in the Deir el Shein direction from south of Ruweisat Ridge. However the German advance was not ended and the two armoured brigades had to fight where they stood, south of the ridge. Dusk brought an end to the fighting which does not seem to have been particularly destructive. At the end of the day the DAK was down to 26 tanks. More British tanks now had the 6-pdr which, along with the American 75-mm, extended the range of tank engagements. The armoured brigades were well supported by the guns of 7th Motor Brigade, as the German tanks were further away and could not harass the gunners with MG fire as they did previously. Auchinleck, who had watched 2nd Armoured Brigade going into action, noted that this day saw a general improvement in artillery tactics in 8th Army. At the end of the day 1st Armoured Division was back in XXX Corps.

Next day saw little change. The two armoured brigades stood just to the south of Ruweisat Ridge, the Germans attacked but were held fairly easily. The 9th Lancers, containing a squadron from 4th Hussars, arrived with a wide variety of tanks as a reinforcement for 22nd Armoured Brigade. They were immediately thrown into the fight. The composite Bays and 4th Hussars squadron was in action north of Ruweisat Ridge losing several tanks and the squadron leader, Major Viscount Knebworth of the Bays. At the end of the day the two armoured brigades had 38 Grants, 61 Stuarts, 8 Cruisers and 12 Valentines.

The next day, 4th July, seemed to show that the Germans were pulling back, but when the two armoured brigades tried to follow up they ran into an AT screen, this stopped them but overnight 1st KRRC carried out an attack which destroying several AT guns, a hint as to what night fighting might have been able to achieve. A Jock column from 7th Motor Brigade managed to evade axis units and get behind their line and shell the Fuka airfield. This column would have been much better employed with the armoured brigades shelling the *pakfront*[2] Next day General Lumsden concluded that his division was played out. He had a short but stormy interview with the corps commander demanding the division's relief. He did not get it, but this event does illustrate why there was a pause in operations for a few days. These lulls were very much a characteristic of the desert campaigns.

On 8th July the 2nd Armoured Brigade was brought forward to come under XIII Corps and over the next few days there was yet another reorganisation. The division took over 2nd Armoured Brigade, but 4th Armoured Brigade and 7th Motor Brigade went to 7th Armoured Division. The Wall Group was set up, this was a temporary and highly flexible organisation consisting of what units were available at the time, under Brigadier RB Waller.

1st Armoured Division, Major-General H Lumsden
    2nd Armoured Brigade, 46 Grants, 11 Stuarts and 59 Cruisers, Brigadier R Briggs
        9th Lancers, including one squadron RGH
        3rd/5th (Composite) RTR
        6th RTR, including one squadron 10th Hussars
    22nd Armoured Brigade, 31 Grants, 21 Stuarts and 23 Cruisers, Brigadier WG Carr
    Royal Scots Greys
    3rd County of London Yeomanry
The Wall Group, principle units only
    One composite Guards Battalion
    One battalion Essex Regiment
    One battalion Rifle Brigade
    Northumberland Fusiliers, detachments only
    The Buffs, detachments only.
    Eight field batteries.

The division came under XIII Corps and was posted at Deir el Hima, but the Wall Group was sent to support XXX Corps. Late on 14th July 22nd Armoured Brigade moved to Alam Nayil following reports of axis tanks in that area.

As soon as possible General Auchinleck ordered a major counterattack. The essential part was that a brigade of XXX Corps was to capture Point 64, roughly in the middle of Ruweisat Ridge, and two New Zealand brigades of XIII Corps were to capture the western half of the ridge. The 4th NZ Brigade was to be on the left, at Point 63. The three brigades were to be supported by the two armoured brigades of 1st Armoured Division, 22nd in the south and 2nd in the north. The 1st Armoured Division's 'Wall Group' was to support the XXX Corps.

This action is usually referred to as 'First Ruweisat'. It was not to be a triumph for the 1st Armoured Division.

The infantry attack was to take place on the night of 14/15th July. The most important brigade attack, and the one involving the longest approach march, of six miles, was that of 4th NZ Brigade. The brigade jumped off at 11.00 pm and was broadly successful but one battalion was badly scattered and some enemy posts were by-passed which prevented ammunition resupply. Worse, the division's artillery was so far back as to be out of range. The ground was rocky making it almost impossible to dig in.

At dawn, 4.45am, on 15th July the brigade was surprised to find that there was a company of German tanks roughly a mile to the south. These tanks attacked the battalion closest which was in a very vulnerable position with no ammunition resupply or heavy weapons coming forward. It had only four AT guns on their portees, they were soon knocked out and the bulk of the battalion surrendered. As can be imagined the New Zealand brigadier, Kippenberger, was extremely irate that the British tanks, which he had been counting on to cover his flank, were missing. He contacted his divisional commander and then went to see General Lumsden and

Brigadier Briggs. The interview can be imagined. As the New Zealand Official History put it, '*It was small wonder that 4 Brigade, indeed the whole Division, was for a long time very bitter about anybody who wore the black beret.*'[3]

The problem was in badly drafted orders at corps level, which stated that: '*The 1st Armoured Division was to protect the left flank of the New Zealanders from first light on the 15th July*', to quote the Official History. However in the orders issued by General Lumsden the armoured brigades were only ordered to '*be prepared to move*' to provide this support, but would only actually do so on receipt of a direct order. The Official History stated that this reflected the armoured forces dislike of being shackled to infantry units and the fact is that to provide significant support at dawn was always going to be very difficult. No doubt the extent of this difficulty was not appreciated by the infantry, but even though the tanks could come up with many reasons for their failure there must be a lingering suspicion that the tanks showed a lack of enthusiasm for the task. Perhaps it was a case of pure fatigue increasing the friction of war. In this circumstance it may be wondered if General Lumsden's preference for verbal orders should have been replaced by a rather more formal system.

Presumably as a result of the Kippenberger-Lumsden interview, at 7.00 am 2nd Armoured Brigade moved off in a north-westerly direction to assist the 5th Indian Brigade whose attack had stalled. Two of the armoured regiments were to be halted by mines and AT guns, but the third escorted a battalion on to Point 64 by 10.00 am.

Remarkably 22nd Armoured Brigade did not immediately move north, but seems to have spent the day, alongside 7th Armoured Division, skirmishing with axis troops to the south. Later in the day the 3rd CLY moved forward and took up a position fairly close behind the New Zealanders, but because some German tanks had been sighted at Deir el Shein, it was not sent to assist the infantry. The result of its absence was tragic. At 5.00 pm the Germans mounted a counter-attack from the west on to Point 63. The result was the destruction of 4th NZ Brigade. At 6.15 the brigade HQ was captured, but German progress east was halted by 2nd Armoured Brigade and the Indians.

Night put an end to the fighting. Next morning after another German attack had been held the defending tanks were reorganised and a squadron, a few other crews and all others tanks of the 3rd CLY were transferred from 22nd to 2nd Armoured Brigade. The remaining CLY personnel were withdrawn. Then, at 7.30 pm, another, more serious, German attack was put in against the Indians. However by this time an AT battery of 16 6-pdrs had been brought forward and dug in. The Germans attacked out of the setting sun, which was blinding the gunners so smoke was fired behind the tanks so as to silhouette them. The Germans seem to have missed the AT guns and concentrated their fire on the Grants of 2nd Armoured Brigade which stayed at long range. The result was the destruction of 24 German tanks and several other AFVs with insignificant losses among the British and Indians.

This action concluded this phase of the fighting. The three days had been a disaster for the New Zealanders, total casualties, including missing, for the division were 1,405. Not surprisingly they blamed 1st Armoured Division for this.

By 18th July General Auchinleck felt ready to try again, and there can be little doubt that the armoured balance had tilted in the British favour:

1st Armoured Division had 61 Grants, 31 Stuarts and 81 Cruisers,
7th Armoured Division had 4th Light Armoured Brigade of armoured cars and Stuarts,
and 23rd Armoured Brigade had arrived, with approximately 132 Valentines and 18 Matilda IIs. This brigade came directly under XIII Corps. Wall Group was disbanded.

The German situation, of which Auchinleck was at least partly aware, was difficult. They had less than 50 serviceable tanks, and around 100 tanks awaiting repairs. The Italians had around 50 serviceable. Consequently General Auchinleck gave orders for the next action to start on the evening of 21st July. It was to be known as 'Second Ruweisat'. Perhaps planning might have been less ambitious if General Lumsden and Brigadier Briggs had not been wounded on 18th July. Lumsden's replacement, Gatehouse, took over the division on 19th July by which time everything was settled.

The essential part of this operation was to be undertaken by XIII Corps, in Phase 1 two infantry divisions were to break through the German front. To the north 5th Indian Infantry Division was to capture Point 63 at the western end of Ruweisat Ridge, and Deir le Shein; to the south the NZ Division was to advance to the eastern edge of the El Mreir depression. Phase 2 was to see armoured troops exploit to the west. This simple plan was to be greatly complicated by extensive minefields.

In Phase 1, 2nd Armoured Brigade was to be on hand to ward off counter-attacks against the New Zealand infantry after they had gone firm on their objectives. 22nd Armoured Brigade was to protect the left, southern, flank of the New Zealanders.

Phase 2 was planned to start at 8.0 am with an advance along the boundary between the two infantry divisions by 23rd Armoured Brigade. It was to hold an area six miles behind the German front line with two Valentine regiments until 1st Armoured Division could drive through. There was an obvious similarity between this operation and Operation Supercharge, but that, and other operations were to show how difficult it was to get a pursuit started. In view of this it is plain that this aspect of the battle had not been properly thought through.

Phase 1 was the immediate concern of 1st Armoured Division and everyone involved could be expected to be determined not to repeat the mistakes of the first Ruweisat Ridge battle. The New Zealanders knew how difficult it would be to move their AT weapons forward and that soon after dawn they could expect to be counter-attacked by German tanks so they agreed to the plan on the basis that, at dawn, the 1st Armoured Division would be on hand to keep the panzers off. Following discussions the New Zealanders quite reasonably believed that this was confirmed at army, corps, division and even brigade level. But alas for plans!

The operation started well, artillery preparation was good and the New Zealanders reached their objectives at 2.45 am on 22nd July. The German tanks, not, like the British, refusing to move at night, drove to counter-attack positions and, aware of the importance of timing, attacked as soon as visibility allowed, at around 4.30am.

Once again the New Zealanders did not have the means of defending themselves against tanks, the ported AT guns were soon destroyed and the leading brigade was overrun, with a total of 700 casualties. 2nd Armoured Brigade was not on hand to hold the German tanks off. The brigade commander had insisted that his tanks could not move at night so they could not get forward fast enough to engage the Germans and neither corps nor division saw fit to order otherwise. One of the 2nd Armoured Brigade regiments, 3/5 RTR, was on Ruweisat Ridge so not involved. When the other two regiments did move they were delayed by mines and, when they were finally through, 6RTR came under AT gunfire, lost three tanks and pulled back, but that was mid morning, far too late to achieve anything. Although 22nd Armoured Brigade managed a long range exchange of fire with the Germans it also achieved nothing.

At 6.25 am General Gatehouse requested the Corps Commander to delay Phase 2, but this request was turned down because of the belief that the Germans were rattled. However it was agreed to move the centreline of the 23rd

Armoured Brigade's attack south by one mile as the Indians were making only slow progress and were not clearing the mines they were expected to. Unfortunately this message was not received by 23rd Armoured Brigade, which at 8.30 am went storming in with two regiments up, through the minefield towards a *pakfront*. It was nearly wiped out. Fortunately its third regiment was attached to an Australian division and was not involved in this disaster. The German counter-attack reached Point 63 before Rommel called it back. General Gatehouse was wounded at 9.00 am and Brigadier Fisher took over temporary command.

The Valentine tank was originally designed as an infantry tank even though it did not have the armour of Matilda II or the later Churchill. However, the Valentine's armour was as good as anything 2nd Armoured Brigade had, and even if it meant delaying the attack a day or two deploying 23rd Armoured Brigade in support of the New Zealanders and keeping 2nd and 22nd Armoured Brigades for any possible breakthrough would have seemed more sensible than the course taken.

Regardless of how the performance of the 2nd Armoured Brigade was regarded, the difficulty in moving tanks through a minefield and in emerging from the lanes and deploying in the face of the enemy were important lessons to learn for Operation Lightfoot.

There was to be one more action before the battle became static, it was to be called 'Operation Manhood'. The action was to be in the north, XXX Corps was to drive a lane through the minefields in the Miteirya Ridge area, and 2nd Armoured Brigade, followed by 4th Light Armoured Brigade from 7th Armoured Division, would surge through and exploit westwards.

The infantry attacked on the night of 26th/27th July and the result was near chaos. Some infantry did advance beyond the mines but attempts by the tanks to reinforce them failed. 6RTR was the only regiment from 2nd Armoured Brigade to see any action but it could not get through the minefield being under AT fire. The infantry were overrun by the counter-attack.

This series of actions showed that, although infantry could attack at night and pass through a minefield, tanks would have a great problem in following them through in the same night. If the tanks could not do this, the infantry would be vulnerable to an armoured counter-attack. Although these operations collectively achieved their purpose of halting Rommel's troops, individually they were failures and pointed the way to the difficulties to be overcome in Operation Lightfoot.

The brief account given here of the period between, and including, Operations Aberdeen and Manhood has hardly conveyed the apparent administrative chaos as regiments were switched from brigade to brigade as they were pulled back to refit then, coming forward again, were sent where then need was greatest. Likewise squadrons could be attached to different regiments. An extreme case was the 10th Hussars at the end of August which had three sabre squadrons, none of which was 10th Hussars, and at this time the regiment was in 7th Armoured Division. All this must have looked like chaos but the staffs involved never lost control. Even so is quite possible that the return to more orderly organisation was one of the factors resulting in much improved morale when General Montgomery took over 8th Army.

There is no doubt that the Aberdeen to Manhood period saw the very nadir of British armour's performance and reputation. This doleful fact may be laid at 1st Armoured Division's door. To some extent the reason for this may be put down to exhaustion. The division had been in almost continuous action from December 1941 to July next year, and depressingly, much of this action was retreating. The New Zealanders in particular had noticed a certain lack of enthusiasm in the division and contrasted this to the keenness shown by the newly-arrived 23rd Armoured Brigade.

However as much as they might have admired this keenness, they would also have noted the casualties the new brigade suffered.

There was probably a reason other than exhaustion for the division's poor performance. The worst of the division's failures were those when it was acting in support of infantry formations. However such operations were not what armoured divisions had been created for. This fact was confirmed in the manual relevant to this period, the Army Training Instructions of May 1941 [4]. This manual lists the roles of an armoured division as:

  i   *Engagement of enemy armoured formations.*
  ii   *Attack of infantry formations unless holding an organized position.*
  iii *An outflanking movement or operations against enemy lines of communication or rear.*
  iv   *Maintenance of the momentum of attack, after a break through.*
  v   *Pursuit.*
  vi   *Reconnaissance in force, including the penetration of enemy screens.*
  vii *Counter-attack in defence.*
  viii *Denial of ground to the enemy during a withdrawal.*
  ix   *Action against enemy airborne forces.*

If these were the activities the armoured unit commanders expected to be involved in, it is not surprising that they were unenthusiastic about combining with infantry, particularly as the armoured division was not equipped with thick-skinned Infantry tanks. This makes the pointless squandering of the Valentines of 23rd Armoured Brigade all the more tragic.

Naturally it should be possible on the basis of common sense to conduct operations outside those prescribed in manuals, but drills and procedures are developed so that a military machine runs smoothly despite the stresses of fatigue, fear and casualties, and when such drills are not in place, or have not been practiced, then when the military machine is stressed it may well not function. That is what seems to have happened to 1st Armoured Division in the actions round Ruweisat Ridge.

Note 1,

TNA WO106/2234 Operations in the Western desert 1942 MAY-JULY: Court of Enquiry Vol I

TNA WO106/2235 Operations in the Western desert 1942 MAY-JULY: Court of Enquiry Vol II

TNA WO106/2236 Operations in the Western desert: Court of Enquiry: Observations by Maj Gen Richie

Note 2,

A *Pakfront* is a defensive line of AT guns. It is also a good example of the way that the Germans invented words to express concepts and make orders easier to pass. It is an acronym-compound word based on *'Panzerabwehrkanone front'*.

Note 3,

Official History of New Zealand in the Second World War, Divisional Cavalry, RJM Loughnan, p201. The New Zealanders seem not to have realised that only the RTR wore the black beret, and they were a minority among tank crews.

Note 4,

ARMY TRAINING INSTRUCTION No 3, Handling of an Armoured Division, May 1941

Chapter 9
The Battle of Alamein

General Montgomery assumed command of the 8th Army on 13th August 1942, and one of his first acts was to organise X Corps, what he referred to as the 'reserve corps'. Originally he wanted it to contain three armoured divisions and an infantry division, but finally it was two armoured divisions, the 1st and the 10th.

The X Corps was to be commanded by General Lumsden, promoted from the command of the 1st Armoured Division, the order of battle of which was:

1st Armoured Division, Major-General R Briggs
    12th Lancers (reconnaissance regiment, armoured cars)
    2nd Armoured Brigade, Brigadier F Fisher
        The Queen's Bays
        9th Lancers
        10th Hussars
        Yorkshire Dragoons (motor battalion)
    7th Motor Brigade, Brigadier TJB Bosville
        2nd Battalion, KRRC
        2nd Battalion, RB
        7th Battalion, RB
    Three Field regiments, RA
    One AT regiment, RA

Each of the tank regiments had an RHQ squadron containing four Crusaders and a troop of scout cars, one sabre squadron of 16 Crusaders and two squadrons each of 15 Shermans. The armoured brigade now had a motor battalion, the Yorkshire Dragoons organised as infantry. This regiment had been mounted on horses until the end of February 1942, being the last horsed regiment in the British army. Then it was moved from Palestine to Egypt to convert to armour, but because of a shortage of real tanks it was employed carrying out deception manoeuvres with dummy tanks, then setting up the last line of defence in Egypt. Finally, at the end of

August, it joined 2nd Armoured Brigade. As the short regimental history puts it *'their main tasks were the taking over of sections of the line from the armour and protection of the tanks by night'*. In the battle and immediate pursuit they suffered a total of 89 casualties.

Also, in September, 7th Motor Brigade joined the brigade. Each of the four motor battalions had 16 6-pdr AT guns and the AT regiment had 64 more. There was a total of 72 guns in the three Field Regiments.

This organisation was very nearly the standard armoured division one which lasted well beyond the end of the war, although actually all armoured divisions varied from it. The 4th and 22nd Armoured Brigades returned to 7th Armoured Division, deployed far away from X Corps. The 2nd Armoured Brigade handed over all its tanks to 22nd Armoured Brigade on 2nd August and the division took up residence at Khatatba camp and, after nine months solidly deployed in the desert, often on active operations, started on a period of intensive training.

The essential aspect of this training and the new organisation was that the brigade group concept was abolished and all the artillery was to come directly under divisional HQ. As Montgomery emphasised, concentrated artillery fire was *'a battle-winning factor of the first importance'.... 'command must be centralized under the C.R.A. so that he can use the divisional artillery as a 72-gun battery when necessary'*. From now on *'Divisions would fight as divisions, and they were not to be split up into bits and pieces all over the desert'*.

The training undertaken by the division centred around gunnery for the new Sherman tanks and mastering a drill for the passage of minefields.

The Sherman's 75-mm gun was equipped with the Azimuth Indicator M19 and this was what allowed the development of what is now known as semi-indirect fire. That is, when the commander can just see the target, but the tank is 'turret down', hidden behind a crest. Naturally this makes the tank very difficult for the enemy to engage, particularly if the tank commander insists on frequently jockeying left or right. However this technique does have the effect of slowing operations down, and using up large quantities of ammunition. This technique was developed by the 1st Armoured Division which went into Operation Lightfoot with great confidence in its tanks and level of training.

Penetrating minefields, and emerging on the other side, was reduced to a drill so that it could be practiced and done at night. It is interesting to note that, despite Montgomery's strictures about 72 gun batteries, for the minefield drill each tank regiment took under command a field battery, an infantry company and other supporting troops.

Operation Lightfoot
The plan for the first part of the operation, in so far as it affected 1st Armoured Division, was that XXX Corps would attack overnight and by dawn 24th October would have reached the objective OXALIC. This involved an advance of roughly five miles. XXX Corps would be followed by X Corps, 1st Armoured Division was the northern of the two divisions and it was allocated a mile wide corridor running along the boundary between 9th Australian Division, to the north, and 51st Highland Division. 2nd Armoured Brigade was to pass through OXALIC and take up a position on PIERSON, roughly a mile further on. The 7th Motor Brigade would then come up and set up an AT screen to the right, and 12th Lancers would surge forward to locate the enemy. Then, if there was no armoured counter-attack, the 2nd Armoured Brigade would move forward a further two miles to SKINFLINT where they would be able to halt any lateral movement of axis armour behind their front.

By any standards this was an ambitious plan, and the corps commander, General Lumsden, doubted that it was practicable. There can be little doubt that this opinion was shared by his division commanders.

The obvious question was 'where was OXALIC'. It can easily be stated that it was the rear of the German gun line which, in its turn, was hundreds, if not thousands, of yards behind the minefields. It would not be easy to identify at night during a battle, and that could prejudice the co-operation of the armoured divisions of X Corps with the infantry of XXX Corps. In fact it is fair to say that throughout Operation Lightfoot there was little in the way of co-operation between the tanks of the armoured divisions and infantry.

Training for the armoured troops started late September with practicing passing through minefields at night. Only two months previously the 2nd Armoured Brigade refused to move at night during the second Ruweisat Ridge battle, now the new army commander just ordered it.

The run up to the battle was characterised by numerous deceptive measures. At the assembly point 'sunshades' were laid out, all in their correct positions, so that the tanks could move in and put the sunshades on and from the air nothing would seem to have changed. Also when the tanks moved forward, they were replaced by dummy vehicles. Storms on the 16th and 17th October looked, for a short time, as if they would disrupt these measures, but the damage caused was repaired in time. Right up to the start of the battle the Germans were ignorant of the British troop movements.

The first troops of 1st Armoured Division to go forward were the Minefield Task Force. This was largely a RE unit, but included a troop from each of the three tank regiments. The task force followed closely behind XXX Corps, it was to clear four lanes, each 16 yards wide, through the mile wide corridor.

The tanks, less their sunshades, left the assembly areas at 9.30pm, 23rd October, and started towards the 'SPRINGBOK' track. In accordance with the plan they were resupplied with fuel here at midnight and they moved forward from this at 2.0 am. They had around seven miles to go to reach the infantry start line. The regimental columns of the brigade were to use three of the lanes through the British minefield, these lanes were illuminated by hurricane lamps in tins with the shapes of, from the north, Sun, Moon and Star cut out. The Bays were to use Sun, 9th Lancers and Brigade HQ, Moon, and 10th Hussars, Star. Each regimental column, though it might vary in detail, was led by the reconnaissance troop, in scout cars, followed by a RE detachment, then two Sherman squadrons, Regimental HQ, a squadron of the Yorkshire Dragoons, a battery of 11th RHA (Priests), and the Crusader squadron.

The brigade was advancing roughly along the boundary between the 51st (Highland) Division and the 9th Australian Division, the Australians to the north. The probably unintended result of this was that the 10th Hussars tended, as they were co-operating with the Highlanders, to fight a separate battle to that of the other two regiments.

At first everything seemed to be working well and the leading troops crossed the old German front line at 4.00 am, 24th October, but from then on things became difficult. By this time the atmosphere was thick with dust which severely hampered what little visibility there was. The minefield was crossed in about 15 minutes, and after 10 minutes the next was entered, but both the Bays and the Hussars were halted, in line ahead, in the second minefield. The infantry had not been able to reach the German main defences as there was third minefield they did not know about, consequently they had not been able to subdue the German AT guns.

At dawn the engineers of the Minefield Task Force were nearly through Sun. As visibility improved a German AT gun hit a RE scout car, but the leading troop of the Bays was able to deploy and neutralise it. At least the depth of the unexpected minefield kept the German guns at long range and, to some extent, the sun was behind the British tanks making marksmanship difficult for the Germans, so two squadrons of the Bays were able to deploy, 'B' squadron to the right and 'C' to the left, although they lost two tanks on mines.

The experience of the Hussars on Star was similar. As dawn broke they received orders from the brigade commander to deploy where they were, that is potentially in the middle of a minefield. Fortunately they found that they were just passed it. Their two Sherman squadrons deployed facing forward, 'A' squadron on the right. They could see the Bays to their right and, around 1,000 yards away to the left, some tanks of 10th Armoured Division. The Crusader squadron deployed covering the left flank. The Crusader squadron of the Bays deployed between the other two squadrons.

Both the Bays and the Hussars engaged some German tanks during the mid-morning. The Germans seem to have been uncharacteristically cautious, perhaps they were impressed by the on-going demonstration of air power, and they stayed at long range. The Bays believed they had knocked out ten tanks of twenty that attacked them.

The two regiments spent most of the day spread out in the open under long-range fire, but the tanks kept moving when the commanders realised they were being ranged on and casualties were low. The 9th Lancers came forward in the early afternoon and deployed between the other two regiments.

In mid afternoon the brigade ordered the armoured regiments to continue the advance, this resulted in two separate actions developing. Most importantly the Bays were informed, at 4.00 pm, that two lanes had been cleared through the minefield so the two Sherman squadrons started up them, 'B' squadron on the right. Predictably they came under heavy fire, 'B' squadron losing four tanks, 'C' losing two. Before the tanks could deploy they were attacked by German tanks from the north-west. After a little uncertainty the two squadrons were ordered by the Colonel to face north, on the far side of the minefield and engage the enemy. It was plain, though, that no significant advance could be made and, after the Colonel had contacted the brigade commander, he ordered the surviving tanks to return which they did, crossing the minefield under cover of a smoke screen.

Once the Bays' squadrons were back through the minefield the regiment joined the Lancers as the counter-attacking tanks had increased in numbers. The fight with them lasted till dark and the Bays believed that 26 Axis tanks were left on the field.

There was a different sequence of events for the Hussars, and it is not obvious why the brigade commander allowed two separate actions to develop. After the overnight infantry assault two companies of the Gordon Highlanders had temporally disappeared. They were found to be on Kidney Ridge and an attack was planned to rescue them. This attack was to be supported by the Hussars, but the minefield was a problem. In this period of the war minefields contained mostly AT mines and were only a limited obstacle to infantry though this was to change later in the war. The Minefield Task Force worked hard but even so the tanks could not pass through the minefield at 3.00 pm when the infantry attack went in. While the tanks were waiting at the edge of the minefield they came under heavy artillery fire and the colonel was wounded but stayed in command until this action was concluded. Once through the mines there was a little confusion due to the poor state of the maps, in fact the Hussars' and Highlanders' version of where Kidney Ridge was varied by 1,000 yards. After this action, and the loss of several tanks on mines, RHQ and 'A' squadron stayed beyond the minefield, and 'B' and 'C' squadrons returned.

The RAF carried out many bombing runs over the German position and these are generally credited with being very accurate, yet the fact is that the German AT guns stayed in action when they should have been easy targets. When the bombers came over the 88s, being AA guns, swung their barrels upwards, giving away their position to the Sherman gunners and artillery FOOs.

The other troops were stuck in the minefield. The reconnaissance regiment, which should have surged through PIERSON and now be scouring the desert looking for the Germans, had yet to cross the old German front line, as was the case with 7th Motor Brigade.

The achievements of X Corps were certainly disappointing, but Montgomery after discussing it with General Lumsden, decided to keep battering away towards PIERSON, though the situation was a little confused by 2nd Armoured Brigade mistakenly reporting that it was actually on this objective. The next day, 25th October, the brigade tried again. The morning was misty and visibility limited. The day started with a disaster. The leading battalion of 7th Motor Brigade, 7th Rifle Brigade, was caught just through the minefields and badly bunched up and it was shelled heavily, troops and transport suffering heavy casualties. As early as possible the Bays and Lancers tried to advance, the Shermans leading, the Crusaders in reserve. Because of casualties the Bays had consolidated their Shermans into one squadron. However they ran into heavy AT gunfire, they believed that the Germans had brought forward some guns over night, and soon took heavy casualties. The Bays lost two troop leaders killed. The two regiments pulled back to their original position. In the afternoon the Bays helped defeat an attack on the Australians to their north. They claimed that 18 Axis tanks were knocked out.

The Hussars, continuing their separate action, planned to attack at 11.00 am, but 50 Axis tanks were sighted close to PIERSON so the attack was postponed. No doubt these were the tanks that the Bays were to engage in the afternoon. At 5.00 pm a single squadron attack was put in with heavy artillery support. One squadron, 'C' squadron, drove straight onto the objective, but the artillery created so much dust that the squadron leader stopped it. Immediately the atmosphere cleared German AT guns opened up and five of the Hussars tanks were knocked out. The squadron returned. This action was undertaken to support a brigade of 10th Armoured Division.

On 26th it was accepted that daylight armoured attacks would not succeed so it was decided to send in 7th Motor Brigade to attack at night with the tanks following up next morning. The Bays and the Lancers had a quiet day, but not so the Hussars. The Highlanders assaulted and captured Kidney Ridge, and the Hussars, who were now down to one Sherman squadron, supported them with copious semi-indirect fire. The night attack of 7th Motor Brigade was to result in one of the more famous actions of the desert war.

Forward of 1st Armoured Division's front was a slight swell in the ground known as 'Kidney Ridge', along the leading edge of which ran PIERSON. To the west of this were two defended areas, SNIPE and WOODCOCK, SNIPE being to the south. The plan for the 27th October was for these two locations to be captured each by a battalion of 7th Motor Brigade, and at dawn 2nd Armoured Brigade would sweep by to the north of WOODCOCK, and another armoured brigade would surge by to the south of SNIPE.

The two battalions had only to advance something like 2,000 yards, but the featureless nature of the desert, the thick dust and the artillery barrage which may not have been on target, all went to make navigation difficult. The difficulty of navigation and the poor state of the maps is illustrated by General de Guingand's comment in his 'Operation Victory' that Kidney Ridge was most likely actually a depression!

WOODCOCK was to be captured by 2nd KRRC. This battalion advanced on time but missed its target and found itself in a vulnerable position to the south of WOODCOCK, so pulled back east a few hundred yards and dug in. The 2nd RB, aiming for SNIPE, also missed its target and finished just to its south, where they dug in. Although the 2nd RB was not actually on SNIPE the fight they had throughout the day is usually referred to as the 'Snipe action'.

The position was occupied around midnight, and was around 900 by 400 yards. It was overlooked by a low ridge 2,000 yards to the south west. The garrison had three companies and 19 6-pdr AT guns, these being 13 from the support company and six from a RA AT battery. A total of 27 guns had started out on the night move but the going was so difficult that eight did not make it. Also, and very unfortunately, the artillery FOO got lost and was absent from the battalion all day. Dawn brought several surprises. SNIPE was very close to lots of Axis armour. In fact a battle group (Stiffelmayer) of 35 AFVs had bumped into SNIPE during the night, and just pulled back until dawn. A reconnaissance party of carriers drove to the south west and discovered the Stiffelmayer group and a laager of Italian tanks. The Stiffelmayer group immediately made off but was engaged by the 6-pdrs at a range of 600 yards, and, being hit on the thin rear armour, lost 16 tanks.

Despite this piece of good fortune the outlook was not very promising. The situation at WOODCOCK was vague and the tanks were late. They should have driven by SNIPE attacking to the north-west at first light but were over two hours late. When they did arrive they proceeded to shell the RB, no doubt because they were not where they were expected to be. Next they tried to advance but came under very heavy fire from German tanks in hull down positions. They lost seven tanks and pulled back, leaving 2nd RB on its own.

The Bays and Lancers were ready to advance before dawn but were instructed to wait as the situation at SNIPE was a little obscure. The two regiments moved forward a few hundred yards at dawn and sent two troops and the reconnaissance troops forward, but German tank and AT gunfire was too intense and they pulled back.

Early in the morning, as soon as its existence and location were sure, the RB came under heavy and sustained artillery fire. Fortunately the low profile of the 6-pdrs and the slight undulations of the ground made accurate shooting difficult, but even so casualties were heavy.

During the morning there was an Italian infantry attack from the south, followed by an attack by 13 Italian light tanks from the west. These attacks seem to have been easily beaten off. They were followed by an engagement with some German tanks moving east to attack some British units to the south of SNIPE. At a range of around 1,000 yards the 6-pdrs of the RB and the British tanks that had pulled back to Kidney ridge knocked out eight of them.

After midday a group of nine Italian light tanks attacked from the south. The situation was becoming desperate. Thirteen guns were still in action but only one was in a position to fire on the attacking tanks, and ammunition was very short. The gun was manned by the Colonel, the platoon commander and sergeant. They held their fire until the attackers were within 600 yards then knocked out six, but by then they were almost out of ammunition. The Lieutenant drove off in a jeep under heavy fire and returned with some. The jeep was hit within ten yards of the gun as the officer returned, but he and the Colonel unloaded it. The remaining three tanks were then knocked out, the last at a range of under 200 yards, but the Colonel was wounded at this moment.

After this there was a lull in the attacks, though the artillery fire did not let up. During this lull the armoured regiments were ordered forward again but this time a troop of Churchill tanks, from an *ad-hoc* unit called 'Kingforce', was loaned to the brigade to help. Unfortunately in this action they were not successful.[1] After this the Bays and Lancers pulled back. Then, around 5.00 pm, 40 tanks of 21st Panzer Division attacked eastwards passing between one and five hundred yards to the north of SNIPE. They were unaware of the existence of the RB position and quickly lost 12 Panzer IIIs and IVs. This caused them to break off the attack and pull back. The division then sent fifteen Panzer IIIs to attack the RB. They advanced cautiously using the ground well. They could be engaged by only three 6-pdrs, these held their fire till the range was down to 200 yards and then destroyed six. This put an end to attacks on SNIPE.

The action had cost the Axis around 50 AFVs, but around a third of the defenders were casualties, mostly caused by artillery fire, and only four guns were still capable of firing. The garrison withdrew at night, which must have looked like a mistake at the time because, just as it left some German tanks drove straight at SNIPE, however they were only moving to escape an artillery barrage, and made no difference.

While it is true that the operation as a whole had been a failure, there had been no breakthrough by the two armoured brigades involved in this action, the rate of attrition inflicted on the axis armour had been very impressive. The 6-pdrs, like the German 50-mm AT guns, had proven difficult to engage, and perhaps, if they had been issued earlier, the Gazala battles might have gone better for the British.

The RB should have been relieved by troops of the 133rd Infantry Brigade of 10th Armoured Division, and as soon as that brigade's commander realised that neither WOODCOCK nor SNIPE were held by British troops he mounted an attack to recapture them. The 4th Royal Sussex arrived at the eastern side of WOODCOCK at 1.30am and was immediately engaged by Axis troops occupying that position. Digging in under fire was not easy in the rocky ground. At dawn 2nd Armoured Brigade moved forward as planned, but Axis tanks were faster and the battalion was overrun before the brigade could intervene. The Official History gives its casualties as 47 dead and 342 missing. Doubtlessly 2nd Armoured Brigade was blamed for this disaster. Some 10th Hussars saw the prisoners being led away but were too late to intervene.

The disaster with the 4th Royal Sussex appears to have been the result of a map reading error, easy enough under the circumstances. Otherwise the deployment of 2nd Armoured Brigade worked well. The Yorkshire Dragoons had gone forward with the infantry to ensure that the tanks would be correctly positioned in the morning and when the attack, supported by 340 guns, had proven a success, the 9th Lancers moved forward at dawn into the locations chosen by the

Yorkshire Dragoons. The Bays moved up at 9.00 am to the right of the Lancers and the 10th Hussars moved up on their left as the divisional boundaries were being adjusted.

After this, this part of the front went on the defensive, which signalled the end of Operation Lightfoot. 1st Armoured Division was relieved by 10th Armoured Division and pulled back to refit and reorganise.

Operation Supercharge
The reason for the pause in the battle was the reorganisation required for Operation Supercharge. This operation was to be similar to Operation Lightfoot but the attacking troops should not encounter the deep minefields which had proven so difficult to overcome. The essential points were that two infantry divisions would attack overnight then, just before dawn, the 9th Armoured Brigade would crash through the remaining opposition regardless of losses. Then would come the 1st Armoured Division to break out into the open.

For 1st Armoured Division the most significant aspect of reorganisation was the taking under command of 8th Armoured Brigade:

8th Armoured Brigade, Brigadier ECM Custance
   3rd RTR
   Sherwood Rangers Yeomanry
   Staffordshire Yeomanry
   One Motor Battalion

Each tank regiment had one squadron each of Grants, Shermans and Crusaders. The Official History gives the total brigade strength for these tanks as: 39, 21 and 47. The equivalent figures for 2nd Armoured Brigade were: nil, 90 and 66.

The infantry assault started early in the morning of 2nd November, and the 9th Armoured Brigade advanced, after a postponement of half-an-hour, at 6.15 am. Predictably they were shot to pieces but had, at least, destroyed some of the

AT screen. For the armoured brigades the move forward had been similar to that before Operation Lightfoot, a long struggle through minefields in the dark and thick dust. As for Lightfoot the Bays were on the right and the Hussars on the left. Again the Bays drove along Sun and the Lancers, Moon. The Hussars had a more complicated route going along three different lanes, Star, Moon and Two bars. Even so, probably as a result of experience with this kind of move, the Hussars were in place by dawn.

As the brigade moved forward the scene was one of disaster, there were knocked out tanks everywhere. There were only 19 9th Armoured Brigade tanks remaining of the 94 that went into the action. These tanks deployed on the northern flank of the breach as a composite regiment and came under 1st Armoured Division's orders.

The brigade took up its usual formation and tried to advance but the leading two tanks were hit and it was obvious that the sacrifice of 9th Armoured Brigade had not resulted in the hoped-for effect of the destruction of the German AT defences. The brigade commander, having driven forward and surveyed the situation, gave orders to stand fast. Inevitably the infantry, who had been fighting over night to open a breach in the German lines, thought that this decision was a little pusillanimous, at least, but actually it was sensible. There was now a salient in the German lines, and one worryingly, for the Germans, close to their main north-south road, so they had to attack it and suffer losses. The resulting attrition would be very much in the British favour.

The plan had been for 8th Armoured Brigade to occupy Tel el Aqqaqir, a slight rise at the southern end of 9th Armoured Brigade's objective. The 2nd Armoured Brigade was to deploy about 2,000 yards to the north-west, and 7th Motor Brigade about 1,000 yards to the north of the Tel. The actual situation was less impressive. The 8th Armoured Brigade did not manage to get into serious action during the day. The 2nd Armoured Brigade was little past its start line, and 7th Motor Brigade was still in the rear. But in terms of attrition this did not matter. The first counter-attack, against the Bays, arrived at 8.00 am from the north, 'shortly after this' as the regimental history put it, German tanks on Tel el Aqqaqir started to move forward against the Hussars.

The familiar pattern lasted all day, a long range duel against AT guns, with frequent counter-attacks by tanks, but the brigade could not advance. By midday all forward movement had ceased, the division had lost 14 tanks, with a further 40 'damaged or broken down', to quote the Official History's description. There are, though, indications that many German tanks were destroyed, the Bays claimed that 2nd Armoured Brigade had destroyed a total of 43. This was not as spectacular as a breakthrough but it was disastrous for the Germans.

At 8.30 pm, when it had become obvious that trying to break through with armour would not succeed, General Lumsden decided to switch to infantry, sending 7th Motor Brigade in at 1.15 am next day, 3rd November. The plan was that each of the three battalions was to have a separate objective, the most important was Tel el Aqqaqir. The attack on this had maximum artillery support and was successful even if it did end up some distance away from where it should have, a fact pregnant with disaster. The critical factor in this type of attack was being able to move up sufficient AT guns and dig them in before dawn when the inevitable counter-attack would come. The KRRC achieved this with eight 6-pdrs and they held off a squadron of Italian tanks at first light. The other two attacks to the north of the Tel were not successful, the AT guns could not be emplaced in time and the counter-attacks forced the battalions to retreat. Such operations, particularly at night, require meticulous planning and thorough reconnaissance but there was not time for either and casualties were suffered pointlessly. Also, detrimentally for the reputation of the division, a South African armoured car regiment, believing the British infantry to be on Tel el Aqqaqir, attempted to drive through and came to grief.

The 2nd Armoured Brigade had been expecting to make a dawn attack to capitalise on the infantry's successes, but this order was cancelled at the last moment, no doubt to everybody's relief. The day started in much the same way as the previous one but now the Hussars were starting to make some ground by the Tel, as was 8th Armoured Brigade to their south, progress though was minimal. To try to crack the defence the Sherwood Rangers Yeomanry, one of the 8th Armoured Brigade's regiments, tried a charge and seemed to have some success before being forced to retreat. The day cost the division 16 Grants and Shermans, and 10 Crusaders. This kind of action, with the tanks in turret-down positions using semi-indirect fire, was expensive in 75-mm ammunition and its re-supply was difficult and a major concern. Presumably, though, ammunition was a greater worry to the Germans.

The general failure of this day must have been disheartening for 1st Armoured Division, but this was the day that the Axis retreat started. Unfortunately there was time for another disaster. Towards the end of the day 51st Highland Division was ordered to advance, the leading battalion riding on the Valentine tanks of the division's supporting tank regiment. It advanced assuming Tel el Aqqaqir was occupied by 8th Armoured Brigade. The surviving tanks pulled back, some covered with blood and the corpses of infantrymen. No doubt this was another blow to the reputation of the 1st Armoured Division.

The start of the German retreat had been noticed and, late in the afternoon, the Bays were pulled back and moved to the south of the Hussars ready for an early advance next day.

Next morning the break through came, at first light the Bays stormed through, the Crusaders leading with the composite Sherman squadron following, and the Hussars and Lancers echeloned back to the right. The Hussars captured *en route* General von Thoma, commander of the *Panzerarmee*, who had come forward to see for himself how bad the situation was.

The tanks of both brigades covered around four miles before reaching Tel el Mansfra where they came across a German position, the first Bays tank was hit and the advance halted for the night. This marked the end of Operation Supercharge.

The Pursuit
The battle of Alamein can be regarded as ended on 4th November, the pursuit started the same day. On this day 8th Armoured Brigade reverted to the 10th Armoured Division. The X Corps then contained three armoured divisions, the 1st, 7th and 10th. The 1st Armoured Division was ordered north-west to El Daba on the coast road, the 7th was sent on a long detour in the desert where it ran out of fuel, and the 10th to Galal station about 17 miles further west of El Daba along the coast road.

Early on 5th November the reconnaissance troop of the Bays reported that Tel el Mansfa had been abandoned by the Germans so off sped the brigade in pursuit. They drove in textbook style, the armoured cars of the 12th Lancers out in front, then came the tanks with 10th Hussars leading, the Bays echeloned back to the left and the 9th Lancers to the right. They travelled like this for 22 miles until they were halted by three 88s. The 12th Lancers captured one as it was being limbered up but the other two opened fire and hit two scout cars and a Crusader of the Hussars.

After overcoming the 88s the Hussars hit the coast road at El Daba at 1.00 pm, they turned left and progressed a short way while the rest of the brigade came up then they waited while the fuel wagons of the 'A' echelons caught up, which they did at 4.00 pm. Then, at 5.30 pm the brigade moved off south-west in the direction of Bir Khalda. Seeing that the bulk of the axis forces had escaped, the aim was now to cut them off at Mersa Matruh where it was assumed that Rommel would make a stand. Consequently the brigade was to make a long detour through the desert to the coast road.

The brigade moved over night, driving in single file and following the 12th Lancers. The order of march was: Bays, brigade HQ, 9th Lancers and 10th Hussars. The first part of the march was slowed by the numerous changes of direction required to avoid the old British minefields, though the Bays believed that the Germans could well have lifted the mines to redeploy them at Alamein. Also there were frequent contacts with odd Axis units, in fact some German lorries may have joined to column at one stage. A large marching column of Italian infantry was found, which, having no transport, only wanted to surrender.

There was a halt at 7.45 am, 6th November, after 40 miles, to wait for fuel re-supply. The echelon lorries arrived shortly after 1.00 pm. Unfortunately not all had made it as they had been scattered by an enemy column on the way, so the result was a shortage of fuel. The tanks, particularly the Mk I Shermans, not having been well maintained were using excessive quantities of fuel, and over such heavy going were using three gallons per mile. To get best value for the fuel available the Bays loaned their seven diesel-powered Shermans to the Lancers, and their six Crusaders to the Hussars. The remaining Bays tanks proceeded to Bir Khalda after 3.00 pm when the remaining fuel lorries came, arriving at Bir Khalda at last light.

After refuelling the brigade marched on but it started to rain. By mid-afternoon Bir Khalda was reached and 7th Motor Brigade, which had been following the armoured brigade, dug in there. The armoured brigade continued on until they reached a location 30 miles to the south of CHARING CROSS, a road junction to the south-west of Mersa Martuh where they ran out of fuel. By this time it was raining heavily and there was little chance of the echelon lorries catching them up.

The situation was frustrating. Axis transport could actually be seen in the distance on the coast road but the brigade was not in a position to disrupt it. The next day, 7th November, was the same, the rain still hammered down, and the Axis vehicles still drove west along the coast road. So a plan was hatched to set up a type of Jock column. The tanks were drained of fuel to provide some for a battery of guns and a squadron of Crusaders, but even this plan was cancelled when it was realised that there was not enough fuel to allow these vehicles to return to the brigade with a reasonable safety margin.

Fuel trucks arrived at 10.0 pm and the brigade set off at 4.30 am, 8th November. It cut the coast road at 9.00 am and drove east, but Mersa Matruh was empty, and the Yorkshire Dragoons went in to secure it, they rounded up an Italian general and several hundred prisoners. The pursuit had failed.

There is little doubt that the pursuit was very disappointing. Montgomery blamed the rain, but perhaps pursuing with five armoured brigades (the New Zealanders had two) was too ambitious, particularly when the fuel allocation was not ruthlessly prioritised. Perhaps the pursuit was not pushed ruthlessly enough. There is the impression that with Rommel in command the result would have been much different.

Some might have wondered how it happened that the RAF allowed the Germans to retreat with so few casualties when they were so vulnerable strung out, in daylight, on a single road. Also, as it became known that allied forces had landed in Morocco and Algeria, some might have thought that driving the Germans back towards Tunisia was a little counter-productive.

While the active pursuit may have been over for 1st Armoured Division, the reconnaissance regiment, 12th Lancers, was to see a little more action. On 14th November it formed the basis of a column to secure the Martuba airfield. This was achieved easily and it was all a bit of an anticlimax.

The 1st Armoured Division concentrated close to Mersa Matruh for a few days then, on 11th November the tanks were loaded on transporters and the crews on lorries and set off westwards.

The division moved but slowly, on the 13th November the Hussars sent a squadron of Shermans forward to join in the pursuit but it saw no action and soon the division caught it up. On 14th the division set up at Capuzzo. Here the Bays handed over 14 tanks to the 22nd Armoured Brigade. Then the division progressed to El Adem and Tmimi where it halted.

Note 1

Kingforce was a three tank troop of Churchill tanks from the Special Tank Squadron, named after its commander, Major N King MC of the 2nd Royal Gloucestershire Hussars. Churchills were not yet on general issue but were doing troop trials. Kingforce was not lucky, the gun recoil mechanism of one jammed and the tank had to withdraw, and one was destroyed by gunfire. The story on this one is obscure, after the battle it was found to have sustained 38 hits on its front, six by 75-mm guns, 31 by 50-mm and one HE round. One 75-mm and two 50-mm rounds had penetrated. The rear of the tank had been hit eight times by 6-pdr shot, of these three penetrated the turret, one the gearbox. There are two possible explanations, one, the tank was reversing slowly and would have presented an unfamiliar but basically square profile to the gunners who mistook it for a German, and this was the version believed at the time. Two, the tank was knocked out and burning, the smoke was a nuisance so the tank was shot up to encourage it to burn faster. Tragically only one crewman is thought to have survived and the truth of this incident will never be known. The remaining Churchill behaved well.

Chapter 10
Tunisia

The rest was to last three months. The division had a relaxing and well supplied Christmas then, on 27th December the Hussars were ordered to hand over 36 tanks to 8th Armoured Brigade. Next, due to storm damage at Benghazi and the consequent necessity to carry supplies to the fighting troops in Tunisia from the railhead at El Adem, the division had to surrender most of its transport.

Late in January 1943 there was a large delivery of Crusaders at Benghazi and Shermans at Tobruk so parties from the three armoured regiments were sent to take them over. Finally, with various draughts, the division was up to strength.

Towards the end of February the division was called back to the war. The tanks went on transporters to a staging area to the south of Tripoli. The Hussars went first followed by the Lancers, then the Bays. The RHQ of the Hussars was given the responsibility of running the X Corps tank park. However plans kept on changing and, as the tanks arrived in Tunisia over 100 of them were handed over to 8th and 22nd Armoured Brigades. This was because a German attack was expected at any time and it came on 6th March, known as the Battle of Medenine. 1st Armoured Division was not involved, but the now tankless troops, less the Bays and 7th Motor Brigade which were still en route, were organised into three ad hoc groups to defend the staging area. They were not needed. The Bays arrived later, but still had to give up their tanks.

Over the next few days the remaining troops of the X Corps, and the 2nd Armoured Brigade regiments sent parties to Tripoli to take over replacement tanks, again. The Bays were the last regiment and they drew their tanks on 14th March. Next day they zeroed their guns in the morning, at midday the officers assembled to be addressed by General Montgomery, and at 4.00 pm the regiment moved out to take up its position for the Battle of the Mareth Line.

The Mareth Line was based on the Wadi Zigzaou and was rumoured to be very strong, in fact General Alexander believed it to be as strong as the German defences at El Alamein. The 8th Army closed up to it in February 1943 and on 6th March the Axis had tried a spoiling attack that was defeated at Medenine. The Line was to be assaulted by XXX Corps in the east. The New Zealand Corps was on the left and the X Corps was in reserve behind the New Zealanders. The X Corps consisted on the 1st and 7th Armoured Divisions and a Free French Column. Although the progress of 1st Armoured Division to the Mareth Line had seen no fighting, its progress had been an administrative triumph. The Official History states that moving the division forward required 289 tank transporters and 100,000 gallons of fuel which had to be dumped at nine staging points, a task that required much more fuel to accomplish. The whole corps required 4,795 tons of fuel.

As the New Zealanders moved off to the south-west the 7th Motor Brigade took up a position to the north-west of Medenine facing south to prevent and axis attack rolling up the line. The Lancers were placed in support of this brigade.

On 17th March the division was called on to create a diversion so the Bays and Hussars and the divisional artillery moved off, at 5.00 am, and drove around five miles to the west past the motor brigade and spent the day firing at suspected enemy positions. The 75-mm guns of the Shermans were useful in this role. They caused minimal damage but the exercise was believed to have been worthwhile. After this the Bays swapped with the Lancers.

As the day of the assault on the Mareth Line approached the division edged to the right so as to free up 51st Highland Division to be able to take part in the operation. Anticipating a quick follow up across the Wadi Zigzaou a Route Task Force was set up to clear four routes across the Mareth Line for X Corps to drive through. The task force was to consist of the Bays, Yorkshire Dragoons and engineers but it was not to be used.

On the night of 20/21st March the assault on the Mareth Line commenced, but unfortunately it was a failure. It was renewed the next night with the same result. This was a serious attempt not just a demonstration, and yet while it was in progress the New Zealand Corps outflanked the Mareth Line and, at 11.30 am 21st March the New Zealanders were only 15 miles south-west of El Hamma.

Until early 23rd March the main attack had been across the Mareth Line and the NZ outflanking move the subsidiary one. The 7th Armoured Division was under orders to provide two squadrons for the Mareth Line operation. But by this time it had become obvious that the main thrust had failed, so the New Zealanders' operation became the main one, and 1st Armoured Division was sent off to join them.

Command of the NZ Corps now devolved on General Horrocks, commander of X Corps. This was not popular with the New Zealanders who were probably still a bit suspicious of British armour following the debacles at Ruweisat Ridge the previous July.

The 2nd Armoured Brigade received the changed orders at 10.00 am on 23rd March. Their tanks were loaded on transporters by 6.00 pm and they set off soon afterwards, arriving at Foum Tatahouine, 20 miles away, at 2.15 am. Here they unloaded and continued on their tracks. It was a very difficult march through soft sand and dust storm, and by dusk on 24th March the division had covered 43 mile, a creditable distance under the circumstances, but they still had 30 miles to go and the battle they were moving up for had to be postponed by 24 hours.

The tanks arrived at the forming up place next afternoon, joining with the New Zealand division which was being held up by the German positions on the Djebel Tebaga. On 23rd March General Freyberg received from General Montgomery a proposal to lay on a very heavy aerial bombardment on these German positions, and blast a way through them. Neither Freyberg nor General Horrocks was really that keen on that idea, but Montgomery insisted. The operation was to take place on 26th March. The RAF would pound the Germans during the day, then the New Zealanders, with 8th Armoured Brigade in support, would attack at 4.00 pm. Their first objective was 2,000 yards away, their second, 2,500 yards past that. At 6.15 pm, the 1st Armoured Division, which was to follow close behind the New Zealanders, would pass through them and go on to a forward staging area 3,000 yards further on. Once there they would wait until the moon provided enough light, then around 11.15 to 11.30 pm, they would advance to El Hamma.

The division, at the start of this action, contained 67 Shermans, 13 Grants and 60 Crusaders. The regimental groups were reformed with each of the armoured regiments taking under command a squadron of the Yorkshire Dragoons and a battery of the 11th RHA. The armoured brigade formed up behind the New Zealanders with the Lancers on the right and the Bays on the left. These two regiments were followed by Brigade HQ then all the brigade's 'soft skinned' vehicles formed in five columns, followed by an artillery battery and then the AT squadron of the Dragoons. The tanks of the Hussars covered the left, right and rear faces of this vulnerable mass.

The division only just made it in time. The last vehicles arrived only 30 minutes before the attack was launched. To save time the RASC brought the artillery ammunition right up to the guns instead of the standard, and safer, procedure of establishing ammunition dumps some way to the rear.

The armoured brigade went into action perfectly, passing through the New Zealanders at 6.00 pm, not even slowing down. It came under some AT gunfire but only suffered light casualties. Even so it was it was not making the expected progress until dusk, when the AT gunners found marksmanship more difficult then the tanks surged on to the staging area arriving on time at 7.30 pm. There it waited till midnight, delayed a little by clouds in front of the moon, then set off again towards El Hamma, progress being frequently slowed to a crawl by broken country crossed by wadis. Progress was more difficult for the wheeled vehicles. The five columns travelled independently and when one came across a wadi it was a matter of the leader dismounting and looking for a crossing on foot.

This operation was the first occasion during the war of a major British armoured breakthrough at night, and the Germans were initially rattled, as was demonstrated by the padre of the 9th Lancers who accidentally captured an 88-mm battery. However the German command still functioned well and its reaction was superb, by 3.15 am it had created a *pakfront* of three 88-mm, four 50-mm and four field guns three miles in front of El Hamma. This halted the pursuit which had covered around fifteen miles, the tanks being delayed from putting in an immediate attack by dust storms. Showing plenty of fight some bypassed panzer units tried to attack the rear of the armoured division's column, and twice two squadrons of the Hussars surged to the rear in search of the panzers but found none. The Germans were easily held off by the 17-pdrs of 76th AT Regiment RA, and the tanks of 8th Armoured Brigade which were following up the armoured division.

Although the breakthrough had been impressive the fact was that the failure to pass El Hamma gave the Germans the chance to pull back from the Mareth Line without excessive losses and to that extent the operation was a failure. It may be speculated that the whole operation left Montgomery with two distinct impressions. One was the ability of the RAF to blast a way through field defences for tanks to pass through. Secondly, that armoured divisions were easily halted so not too much could be expected from them.

To keep the offensive moving the New Zealanders were ordered to advance round the eastern side of the El Hamma position. To facilitate this the 10th Hussars were sent round to its west to create a diversion. This they did by driving fairly close and spending several hours shelling the Germans. The Germans responded in kind and were probably glad to be getting rid of surplus ammunition as they abandoned El Hamma over night.

On the following day, 29th March, the brigade passed through El Hamma. Progress was slow, the

Road passed through the oasis which caused congestion and there were mines to be lifted. When the armoured brigade was north of El Hamma it covered four miles and came into action against the retreating Germans.

Resistance seemed, again, to be crumbling. The New Zealanders reached the coast to the west of Gabes and the brigade surged forward in the direction of Djebel Fatnassa, the Hussars on the right, Lancers to the left and the Bays in reserve. Unfortunately progress was slowed by running into a dry salt pan, which is very soft going. Once through this the Djebel was approached but the tanks were driven back by artillery. As it would be difficult to assault a hilly position with tanks alone, the more so as a deep crater had been blasted into the road, so nothing was done until the evening when the 7th Motor Brigade caught up. The 7th RB put in an attack but could make no progress, so 1st Armoured Division had been definitely halted. After two days the division was withdrawn, handing over to the Free French.

The Djebel Fatnassa position was a part of a strong defensive line along the Wadi Akarit, and Montgomery decided that the assault should be carried out by XXX Corps and X Corps, including the New Zealanders, should pass through the breach.

The division's first task was to make a demonstration against the Haidoudi Pass late in the evening of 5th April. This was done by the 7th Motor Brigade. Next day, following the break through, the division was to follow the New Zealand division and make for a ridge 15 miles away. But, alas for plans, the

8th Armoured Brigade had hardly started the breakout when it was held up by a *pakfront* and that stopped the corps. Some soldiers must have wondered why the RAF could not have sorted out a few AT guns. The result was a day of inactivity for 1st Armoured Division.

Early on 7th April it was confirmed that the Germans had abandoned the Wadi Akarit position and X and XXX Corps took up the chase with 1st Armoured Division on the left. It too a long time to thread 2nd Armoured Brigade through the Djebel Fatnassa passes, but around midday the pursuit could start, 10th Hussars leading, the Bays on the left and Lancers to the right. The armoured cars of 12th Lancers could be seen in the distance on the left where they came into contact with the Americans. The advance was impressively fast, covering 30 miles in the afternoon. In the evening a liaison officer from 8th Armoured Brigade to the right approached 10th Hussars requesting assistance for their left hand regiment, 3RTR, which was fighting against a German tank unit which included Tigers. The regiment wanted to help but brigade HQ vetoed this and the brigade laagered where it was.

Next day, 8th April, the enemy had withdrawn so the pursuit was taken up again with orders to halt when the east-west Mahares-Maknassy railway was reached. The Hussars reached this railway and halted, despite seeing some German artillery being limbered up in the distance. The Bays came up on the left close to the village of Metzzouma, and they advanced a short distance past the railway. At 5.0 pm orders were received by the Hussars to capture the village, which was covered by an AT screen. This was bound to be a difficult task to undertake this late in the day. The Colonels of the two regiments agreed on a plan. The Hussars swung round to the left of the Bays who were reasonably well placed to provide fire support, then they charged the village. The operation was not a success, but the lack of light must have made things difficult for the German gunners as the Hussars had no casualties, but a number of tanks became stuck in wadis. Next morning the Germans had left.

The Bays and Lancers continued the pursuit at first light while the Hussars took a little time to collect themselves and replenish. However this worked out quite well for them as the other two regiments had a large number of their tanks bogged down in wet wadis so the Hussars could tell where the hard surfaces were and drive through them.

By this time the pursuit was being conducted by the 2nd Armoured Brigade on the left and the 8th on the right. The 8th had got a little ahead and as the Bays and Lancers came up the 8th Armoured Brigade was engaging a large number of German tanks. The Bays and Lancers formed up on the left and, as the Hussars caught up, they slotted in between them but dusk put an end to this action.

Next morning, the 10th April, the Germans had departed. The 1st Armoured Division concentrated at Bou Thadi awaiting further orders. Its career with X Corps had ended and, on 12th April, it joined IX Corps.

The tanks were loaded on transporters on 14th April and a start was made painting them green. This was regarded as necessary not only because of the requirement for camouflage, the division was leaving the sandy desert for the greenery of Tunisia, but because it was regarded as important to hide the transfer of 8th Army troops to 1st Army from the Germans. Camouflage was not helped by the new requirement to paint five-pointed stars on all vehicles, and these recognition aids certainly did not prevent all amicide aerial attacks. The tanks travelled on the transporters as far as Le Kef, then continued on their tracks to El Krib where the regiments were made up to strength with Shermans from a 1st Army tank delivery squadron. The wheeled vehicles of the division followed around a day later.

On 20th April the division was visited by Lt-Gen Anderson, the 1st Army commander, and General Alexander the commander of 18th Army Group. During the following night the division moved to its assembly area close to Bou Arada.

For the coming battle the IX Corps was commanded by Lieutenant-General JT Crocker, then Lieut-General BG Horrocks, it contained:

1st Armoured Division
6th Armoured Division
46th Infantry Division.

General Horrocks took over command of the corps on 30th April after General Crocker had been wounded when watching a demonstration of the new Projector Infantry Anti-Tank (PIAT).

The IX Corps was a part of 1st Army and it was going to play a major part in the conquest of Tunis. The essence of the plan as it affected 1st Armoured Division was that 46th Division was to capture the Axis position on the western edge of the Goubellat plain, then the 1st and 6th Armoured Divisions were to surge across the plain in a north-easterly direction towards Massicault in the rough vicinity of which it was expected to encounter the mass of German armour.

The breakthrough was planned to proceed in three phases, in the first, to start at 2.0 am, 23rd April, the infantry was to advance 3,000 yards clearing lanes through the extensive minefields. In the second phase, expected to start around 7.0 am, the 6th Armoured Division was to secure the area to the north of Sebkret el Kourzia and the 1st Armoured Division was to advance behind the 6th then swing north. In the third phase the 1st Armoured Division was to advance up Goubellat valley to the left of 6th Armoured Division and separated from it by the Djebel es Srassif.

The infantry attack commenced on time but its timetable was wildly optimistic and its tasks, which should have taken five hours, actually took 33. The 6th Armoured Division was sent forward around midday, but in its turn it advanced only slowly, this had a knock on effect on 1st Armoured Division which by dusk had covered only five and a half miles and lost many tanks in the minefields.

Next day, 24th April, the prospect looked bright, the 2nd Armoured Brigade had to cross a further minefield but after that it was off into the Goubellat valley in high spirits, the Lancers to the right, Bays to the left and Hussars in reserve. However as the history of the Bays comments, the Goubellat valley did not turn out to be the 'tank paradise that had been expected'.

The valley was covered by unfenced cornfields with crops typically three feet high, but it in places six. It was traversed by a series of wadis that slowed progress, as did mines which were scattered in the corn, but the real shock was how good the Germans were at camouflaging their AT guns. On the left the Bays lost three Crusaders to AT guns which had been placed to hit them when they crossed a wadi at the only available crossing place. On the right the Lancers had a similar experience when their Crusaders squadron was shot up crossing a wadi. The squadron of the Yorkshire Dragoons with the Hussars deployed to the right and put down a MG barrage along the right flank but progress had ground to a halt.

The brigade laagered up and next day the corps commander, General Crocker, pulled 1st Armoured Division back behind the 6th and, on 25th April, deployed it alongside that division hoping that attacking with two divisions on a narrow front would be too much for the defenders. Unfortunately the defenders were the Hermann Goring and 10th Panzer Divisions, and they were not going to crumble. The tanks moved back at 2.00 am, then the 2nd Armoured Brigade took over the positions of 26th Armoured Brigade. The hand over went quite well even though the tanks of the two brigades were on different frequencies, and the *Luftwaffe* raided the area while it was seething with the tanks of six regiments. Fighter planes without specialised AT weapons could do little harm to tanks. The 26th Armoured Brigade formed up to the right of 2nd to continue with the attack.

The advance started at around 7.0 am, the Hussars on the right and the Bays on the left. The 6th Armoured Division tanks could be seen taking heavy casualties so the attack was pressed with determination. The Bays came under fire from some German tanks, one of which was a Tiger, which knocked out six tanks. The Hussars on the right pulled forward to give fire support to the Bays and the left regiment of the 6th Armoured Division. The Hussars claimed 11 Axis tanks for one scout car, however when trying to advance to capitalise on this success they had to cross a crest and the first tank over was hit, and that halted the advance. The brigade pulled back and laagered up, sending the Yorkshire Dragoons forward to hold the tanks' previous positions.

The fact was that IX Corps assault had failed. The 6th Armoured Division was pulled back, and 1st Armoured and 46th Infantry Divisions were left in the line, not doing much. For the first two days one regiment maintained the brigade's position during daylight, but it came under heavy artillery fire and it was plain that the German artillery observers were on Bou Kournine. Unless this hill could be captured IX Corps would not make much progress.

The first attempt at Bou Kournine was a night attack by 46th Division. That having failed, the 7th Motor Brigade took over the left, more broken, sector of the front on the night of 29/30th April, and next night it attempted to assault Bou Kournine. Two companies of the 2nd RB were sent in, but they also failed. Thereafter the summit was kept under sporadic fire by 11th RHA and the Shermans. Little more happened and there was a major re-organisation of IX Corps formations commencing on 1st May. The 1st Armoured Division was taken out of the corps and placed in army reserve, its place was taken by 7th Armoured Division.

The operation had certainly been a disappointment but it had inflicted a degree of attrition on the Germans which they could not support.

The newly-structured IX Corps was redeployed in the Medjez el Bab area, and on 6th May made its breakthrough which signalled the start of the Axis collapse. The 1st

Armoured Division was ordered up to cover the right flank of the IX Corps. Preparations were made for a difficult fight, but in the event the Germans had withdrawn, leaving only mines behind.

On 8th May the 1st Armoured Division returned to IX Corps, replacing 7th Armoured Division which was entering Tunis. The task of the corps was to occupy the Cape Bon peninsula and 1st Armoured Division's task was to capture Cretville at the base of the peninsula. This was accomplished over very difficult terrain, there was little fighting which was fortunate as 11th RHA had been loaned to 6th Armoured Division which was fighting hard a little to the north.

Cretville was really the end of active operations in North Africa for 1st Armoured Division. It spent a few days collecting prisoners, and the campaign officially ended on 13th May.

Chapter 11
Interlude in North Africa

For a few days the division relaxed close to Tunis and the sea, and sent detachments to Tunis for the victory parade. Then the division went back east to the vicinity of Tripoli. Going back to the hot and dusty desert was not appreciated. The division stayed there for two months before moving close to the coast.

Delivery was taken of enough Sherman tanks so that now all the armoured regiments were fully equipped with them, and individual and troop training started. Then all the tanks, and many of the other vehicles, were handed over to 7th Armoured Division. General Horrocks told the assembled officers of the division that they would have to wait three months for new tanks.

Orders were that armoured brigade's motor battalions must be either KRRC or Rifle Brigade, so 2nd Armoured Brigade's motor battalion, the Yorkshire Dragoons, was replaced by 1st KRRC and the Yorkshire Dragoons joined 18th (Lorried) Infantry Brigade. This brigade was the new incarnation of 7th Motor Brigade. The Dragoons changed their title to 9th KOYLI, this being a Yorkshire regiment. One company of the 1st KRRC was allotted to each of the armoured regiments.

The division's commander, Major-General Briggs left to become Director Royal Armoured Corps, and was succeeded by Major-General G Galloway. Brigadier Peake took over 2nd Armoured Brigade but was succeeded by Brigadier R Goodbody in January.

The division then moved to Algeria during October, and settled down at Boufarik, about 25 miles south of Algiers. There were wide open spaces there and gunnery could be practiced. Further experiments were held with semi-indirect fire. On 29th November the entire armoured brigade is said to have carried out a shoot, but as the Bays were very short of tanks perhaps some of the squadrons involved were skeleton organisations. The 10th Hussars' account is not precise but hints that there were limits on the numbers of tanks that could be controlled for this type of shoot.

In February 18th (lorried) Infantry Brigade was detached from the division and joined 1st Infantry Division at Anzio. The brigade saw plenty of action. In an attack in March a large part of the Yorkshire Dragoons was cut off and forced to surrender, causing the regiment (battalion) a total of 170 casualties. The brigade returned to 1st Armoured Division in early August.

By April the full complement of tanks had been issued, and the division was transported to Italy. The tanks and the rest of the division were widely separated, the tanks going to Taranto, and the rest to Naples. Once the division had been assembled it undertook intense training in infantry-tank cooperation. The 10th Hussars trained with 1st Infantry Division, a squadron with each brigade. 'A' squadron trained with 18th Brigade which was on loan from 1st Armoured Division. The Bays trained for a short time with 1st KRRC, then its squadrons had to take turns being infantry. The accent with this training was the close support of infantry in deliberate operations, particularly crossing minefields and anti-tank ditches. This period of training was all too short and, early in August, the move forward to the Gothic Line started.

Chapter 12
Components of an Armoured Division

This chapter will consider the functioning of three important integral parts of the armoured division, but, in the case of infantry and artillery, they will only be considered in terms of their cooperation with the tank regiments which inevitably were the core of the division.

Reconnaissance

Throughout the North African campaigns the armoured reconnaissance regiments were equipped with armoured cars and were assigned one to each armoured division. During the 1940 campaign in France reconnaissance regiments were held at corps level, so 1st Armoured Division did not have one, but this changed in 1941 and the division received the 12th Lancers.

A manual[1] described their employment:

The normal role of the armoured car regiment is reconnaissance, which will generally be carried out directly under the divisional commander. Once the presence of the enemy is suspected the only place for the armoured car regiment is in contact with the enemy, until the full armoured action develops, when it should be withdrawn either to the flanks or to the rear. Its action must not be restricted by limiting its distance in advance of the armoured division. Its task is complementary to that of air reconnaissance, and it is essential that it should be kept fully informed of the work of the Tac.R aircraft operating with the division.

The armament - which includes anti-tank weapons - and the armour of an armoured car regiment enable it to fight for information against minor opposition if its freedom of movement is unrestricted. If it is road bound its powers of reconnaissance are very considerably reduced. Its presence ahead or on the flanks will never relieve other units of responsibility for their own protection.

This organisation was successful in the desert for medium range reconnaissance, the individual armoured regiments being given their own scout car troops for close reconnaissance. There was a constant wartime evolution in reconnaissance procedure, during the 1940 campaign in France the reconnaissance troops were held in two Light Armoured Reconnaissance Brigades, or came directly under the BEF, and 1st Armoured Division had none. For fighting in Europe in 1944 and 1945 the armoured cars were replaced by tanks. Armoured cars continued to be operated by the Reconnaissance Corps, but that was not of interest to 1st Armoured Division. The desert fighting was a point in this evolution, but it made a disproportionately great impression on the troops involved and the army in general, an impression which, it could be argued, still exerts an influence on the design of British AFVs.

The 12th Lancers landed in Egypt on 25th November 1941. The regiment was equipped with 63 Humber armoured cars, which carried a 15-mm gun, and a troop of 10 scout cars. Scout cars were unpopular in the regiment following experience on exercises in England, but this was to change. Scout cars were one of the unsung heroes of the war, and the Daimler Dingo was one of the very few AFVs to stay in production throughout the war.

The armoured cars were organised, as were tanks, in regiments of three sabre squadrons of five three-car troops. In Africa each squadron HQ had one, or more, lorries carrying fuel. These were called 'fighting lorries', and large numbers of them were lost to air attack.

The Humbers were equipped with the Wireless Set No 11 which, vehicle-borne, could give a maximum range for voice of 16 miles, which was not really sufficient, but they were soon replaced by the Wireless Sets No 19 which gave a similar range but were much better in every other way.

After only a few days the regiment proceeded to the desert to join 7th Armoured Division which was in the throes of

Operation Crusader. It stayed under the command of this division until 24th December when it joined 22nd Armoured Brigade shortly before it returned to 1st Armoured Division. Soon after the brigade was sent to try a wide flanking movement south round the German positions at Agedabia.

The regiment, with its squadrons ranging widely to the front and flanks of the brigade, saw plenty of action and lost 10 armoured cars, one of which was recovered. The flanking movement failed, mostly because of lack of fuel and the 12th Lancers returned to join with 11th Hussars to form a screen running from Agedabia to El Haseiat, the Lancers to the left, to cover 1st Armoured Division which was taking over from 7th Armoured Division.

The Germans pulled back to Agheila. The regiment followed up in a thick sand storm to take up a position 80 miles in front of the 'B' echelon. The ground was very rough and that, along with constant attack by the Luftwaffe, made the regiment difficult to supply. Worse, the rough going resulted in the regiment soon being down to two eight car squadrons. The Humbers had a reputation for being under-engined. This rate of attrition was to be fairly typical for operations in North Africa. On 20th January the regiment was pulled back to Msus then, leaving behind one *ad-hoc* squadron of the best running cars under XXX Corps, the rest of the regiment pulled back to the desert railhead, about 80 miles east of Tobruk, to refit and draw new armoured cars from depots in Egypt.

On 25th January the Germans struck and Msus was evacuated rather precipitously. The squadron drove to Mechili and joined XIII Corps, then rejoined the rest of the regiments after a few weeks.

Soon the regiment re-deployed to the desert, under almost continual air attack, watching the German build-up. This was during the lull between Operation Crusader and the Gazala battle, and the regiment was hardly associated with 1st Armoured Division but came directly under XXX Corps. It cooperated with the Royals and a South African armoured car regiment to watch a line running roughly from Gazala to Mechili. It was backed up by a column from the Guards including eight Valentines and some artillery. This lasted till 1st May when the regiment was withdrawn except for 'C' squadron which, having been given the best of the regiment's armoured cars, joined 22nd Armoured Brigade at Bir Harmat, and it was there when, on 27th May, the Gazala battle started.

When news of the German attack was received, just after the morning stand-to, the armoured cars drove to their emergency stations to the west of Knightsbridge. However the Germans came from the south and the situation soon became confused. As the battle progressed the squadron was broken up, troops going to each of 2nd, 4th and 22nd Armoured Brigades, 1st Army Tank Brigade and an infantry brigade to act as radio stations. Then it spent a few days with 7th Armoured Division until relieved by 'A' squadron, which returned to the fighting under 1st Armoured Division, and formed a part of the armoured car line of observation to the north and west of the Knightsbridge Box with the Royals and the South African armoured cars.

There was a pause in the fighting while the Germans assaulted Bir Hachiem. Then, on 11th June, the Germans moved north towards Acroma and El Adem, opposed by 1st Armoured Division. As the division was forced back so were the armoured cars, and 'A' squadron finally returned to the regiment at Capuzzo. The regiment was then attached to 10th Indian Division, except for 'C' squadron, just back from Egypt, which stayed with 1st Armoured Division and covered the rear of 22nd Armoured Brigade as it retreated almost to the Alamein position. *En route* the Colonel was captured, he mistook the nationality of a column of vehicles he approached. Easily done when the Germans were using many British vehicles captured at Tobruk. The squadron came under command of the Royals for a period during the retreat, then spent some time with 7th Armoured Division. As the armies became static the armoured cars were involved in stationary patrols watching the enemy watching them.

The regiment returned to 1st Armoured Division in September 1942 when that division was a part of X Corps and training for Alamein. During the battle there was little call for armoured cars, but once Operation Supercharge had shaken the German front and 1st Armoured Division was out in the open the three sabre squadrons fanned out in front of the division in the approved manner. It had been planned that the reconnaissance regiments would burst through the axis front line and cause chaos among their transport, but in the event only the Royals managed this. Unfortunately the regiment, along with the rest of the pursuing force, was bogged and halted by heavy rains. This disappointment was compensated for by the regiment forming the basis of a column, under the command of 7th Armoured Division, which included artillery, engineers and 240 lorries, which raided 200 miles to the west to capture the Martuba airfields. This successful operation, though unopposed, was a significant achievement. The regiment then went to 7th Armoured Division where it stayed until the breakthrough at the Tebaga Gap.

During this period the regiment was equipped with Daimler armoured cars. These vehicles were a great improvement over the Humbers even if the regiment still regarded them as underpowered. They carried a 2-pdr gun and the Wireless Set No 19. Regimental and squadron HQs retained their Humbers which, being roomier, were better for command purposes.

At the Tebaga Gap the regiment covered the flanks of 2nd Armoured Brigade, but after that armoured cars were of little use in the broken, often mountainous, country of Tunisia where it was difficult to deploy off the roads and so impossible to set up an armoured car screen. As 1st Armoured Division saw little action in that country perhaps this did not matter that much and soon it would be of no interest at all because, in April 1943, the armoured divisions lost their armoured car regiments, which were transferred to the Reconnaissance Corps, and gained an armoured reconnaissance regiment, in effect another tank regiment.

The decision to replace armoured cars with tanks, that is accepting that reconnaissance regiments would have to fight for their information, would seem to fly in the face of the British preference for *reconnaissance by stealth*, but, although it has been suggested that this change may have really been a subterfuge to get another armoured regiment in the armoured division, it was most likely a sensible reaction to the lack of mobility of armoured cars. These vehicles were useful for maintaining a static screen but they could not move fast enough to keep in front of the tanks in an advance. The same problem was experienced in the 1991 Gulf campaign when the reconnaissance regiment was mounted on tracked vehicles, Scimitars, which were more mobile than wheeled vehicles, but still could not outpace tanks.[2]

It is of interest to note that when 12th Lancers left the division their organisation was changed to that of four sabre squadrons of five troops containing two scout cars and two armoured cars. The squadrons each had two self-propelled 75-mm guns and an infantry platoon. Plainly serious fighting was expected.

In North-West Europe the armoured reconnaissance regiments were equipped with Cromwells, these being lower and faster than Shermans. Cromwells were not available in the Mediterranean theatre so the 4th Hussars, the regiment allocated to 1st Armoured Division, was equipped with a mix of Shermans and turretless (sawn-off) Honeys. How sensible this organisation would be for the Italian campaign would be decided on the basis of experience.

The Motor Battalion
There can be no doubt that the record of the motor battalions was disappointing. The reason for this was that, while other armies regarded their mobile infantry as roughly the partners of tanks, the British army believed that the Motor Battalions were there only to provide local security so that the tank crews could get a night's sleep.

An armoured division contained, in its final form, two types of infantry: the motor battalion and the lorried brigade. The three battalions of the lorried brigade travelled in the usual three-ton lorries, known as 'troop carrying vehicles', TCVs, and were in all respects conventional infantry. The motor battalion, on the other hand, travelled in 15-cwt trucks, one allocated to each section. Because of the permanent allocation of vehicles the motor battalion was classified as being 'tactically mounted'. This was quite important because when the soldiers went into action on their feet they could leave their non-essential kit on the trucks. Each company of motor infantry had a platoon of 'Bren gun' carriers which added greatly to its effectiveness.

The motor battalion, then, was a class of infantry unique to armoured divisions. A manual of 1943[3] defined its roles:

1 In addition to the normal functions of a fighting unit, the chief roles of a motor battalion, in cooperation with other arms, are:

   a) To seize and hold ground vital for the manoeuvre of the remainder of the armoured brigade, or to fight a delaying action.
   b) To deny or hold an antitank obstacle against enemy armoured fighting vehicles.
   c) To protect armoured vehicles when halted, or at rest, during the night, by vigorous patrolling and harassing of the enemy.
   d) To carry out close reconnaissance or local protection in front or on the flanks of the armoured brigade, eg as part of an advanced guard when the armoured brigade is leading.
   e) To mop up, to a limited extent, and hold until relieved by the infantry brigade, ground captured by the armoured brigade.
   f) To protect administrative echelons, and observation posts, and gun positions of artillery working with the armoured brigade.
   g) To keep contact with the enemy when, owing to the

necessity for rest or maintenance, the armoured regiments are unable to do so.

2 There are many other tasks that may be visualised for the motor battalion, such as effecting a crossing over an obstacle; establishing a small bridgehead; pursuit; ambushes; removing mines; protection of maintenance parties, etc, or a defile; and possibly, in some circumstances, long distance or medium reconnaissance.

3 When organized enemy opposition, requiring a deliberate attack by infantry, is met, the infantry brigade will usually be employed.

Attacks by the motor battalion or companies will, therefore, be confined to those against a position where a minor degree of resistance only is expected.

Such situations may occur in the early stages of contact; or when the advance of the armour is held up and it is necessary to restore the momentum by overcoming resistance at some definite and limited objective; or when seizing a vital area of ground.

4 In order to carry out its tasks effectively a motor battalion or company (when working independently of the battalion) must have artillery support.

On the subject of the motor battalion cooperating with the armoured regiments of the armoured brigade the manual continued:

1 The motor battalion will, as part of the armoured brigade, always be in close touch with the armoured regiments, and will fight in close cooperation with them:-
  In an advanced guard;
  In a regimental group formed of all arms for some independent role;
  In the deliberate attack by the brigade;
  In delaying actions and counterattacks.

Companies will frequently be placed under command of an

armoured regiment, particularly in close country where motor infantry cannot quickly be moved to support the armour.

2 It is very important, therefore, that personnel of motor battalions should understand the characteristics of the tanks with which they are going to fight and the tactics of armoured regiments. The first essential is recognition of our own tanks.

3 The closest liaison during training should be aimed at. For this reason, the same company should generally be allotted to an armoured regiment so that officers and men get to know each other intimately. Whenever possible, representatives of motor battalions, particularly officers and NCOs, should travel in tanks during the exercises. Personnel of motor battalions should be trained in riding on the outside of tanks, since on occasion it may be a useful method of carrying them to the battlefield, if not under heavy fire. Officers and NCOs of armoured regiments should attend exercises held by the motor battalion in order to understand the infantryman's problem, and advise on the armoured regiment's aspect.

4 When working in close cooperation with tanks the principle should be that where the opposition is anti-tank artillery or pillboxes, buildings etc, the tanks provide the firepower and the infantry the assaulting force. Tanks can move rapidly to a flank and allow the infantry to attack frontally or from the opposite flank. When the ground is suitable and the opposition can be overrun, the tanks may assault, but they should be closely followed up by the men on their feet to destroy the enemy before he recovers from the shock of the tank attack. Supporting fire from light machine guns and mortars, as well as artillery, must be provided for the tank attack.

As can be seen the motor battalions were to be very busy. The list of their roles is impressive but little effort was expended in making them more able to fulfil them. Only in 1944, when American half-tracks became available, was any attempt made at cross-country mobility and even then the armour on these vehicles was negligible.

The first motor battalion was 9th Battalion, Rifle Brigade. This was replaced before Operation Lightfoot by the Yorkshire Dragoons. This, in its turn, was replaced by 1st KRRC at the end of the North African campaign.

The Yorkshire Dragoons were on horses in Palestine until 1942. They were the last operational regiment on horses in the British army. They had a rather chequered history before becoming a motor battalion. Remarkably a number of cavalry and yeomanry regiments, because of lack of armoured vehicles, were mechanized onto pickup trucks but, although it might be thought that such regiments were naturals for the motor battalion role, no attempt seems to have been made to employ them as such. It seems that the army decided that only 'the black and green' had the dash to manage such an exacting role and, in this case, the social cachet to be acceptable to a regular cavalry brigade.

Regardless of who the motor battalion was, and how exhausting its duties were, the battalion achieved little apart from following the tanks and providing overnight security, although that, of course, was very important, though it may be thought that the battalion's 16 AT guns could have been more effectively used.

Artillery
This section is primarily concerned with the employment of artillery in direct support of tanks. This took the form, usually, of a regiment of 25-pdrs which came under the command of the armoured brigade HQ. Such support was found to be necessary because the British tanks of the period were armed with 2-pdrs for which there was no high explosive ammunition so they could not effectively engage dug-in infantry or, writing in broad terms, anything other than tanks which the tanks' MGs could not cope with.

The common procedure was for a battery, that is eight guns,

to be attached to each of the armoured regiments. The Forward Observation Officer (FOO), who was usually the battery commander, would travel in an Armoured Observation Post (AOP) which was usually a 'Bren gun' carrier carrying two radio sets, and he would be in radio contact with the battery which followed behind the tanks. As the war ground on it became common for each battery to have two AOPs.

The design of the AOP varied throughout the war. The carrier was not popular but at least it could deploy with the tanks. Some FOOs preferred to use a truck driven off to a flank, and hope that the Germans would ignore it, finding the British tanks to be more profitable targets. Gun tanks were tried but the FOO had to double as the tank commander which was not practicable. Then armoured cars, commonly Marmon Harringtons the AOP version of which had three radio operators. The final stage of development was a tank stripped of its main armament, but with a dummy gun fitted in its stead. If a tank stood out, for example by having extra antennae, it was made a priority target by German gunners. At the end of the war most FOOs were in sawn-off Honeys.

When a worthwhile target came into view and range the FOO would report that to the battery which would unlimber and come into action if it was decided to engage the target. In theory the AOP and the battery advanced on the same bearing and at a known distance from each other, consequently the indication for the first round, one gun firing, was easy to give. Supplying corrections was easy, and all modern RAC B1 operators are trained to do it. Once on target the whole battery would fire until the end of the engagement.

When it worked perfectly this system was very effective and good for the morale for the tanks crews who were only too well aware of the inadequacies of the 2-pdr. There were, though, weak points. The first was the poor state of radio communications and in a fast moving tank action no other means of communications worked. Secondly was the fact that the guns were towed. Although the gunners became very slick at bringing the guns into action, there was always a time lag, even though finding space to deploy was easy in the desert.

The disadvantage of towed guns was particularly unfortunate since a self-propelled gun had been developed, some of which were issued, on an experimental basis, in 1925. This was the Birch gun, a self-propelled 18-pdr. It might be thought that the Tank Corps would have seized upon the Birch gun as representing a dramatic increase in the firepower of tank formations. Also it might be thought that the infantry would have shown a great interest in it as, perhaps with a different main armament, it could have been developed into a first class tank destroyed, predating the *panzerjager* by many years. Unfortunately neither of these happened and the Birch gun concept was allowed to die.

The need for self-propelled artillery in the desert was obvious, an attempt was made to supply it by mounting a 25-pdr on a Valentine hull, it was to be called the 'Bishop'. The result was not a great success, but was enough of an improvement on a towed gun to ensure that more, and better, self-propelled guns were issued. The Bishop had the gun in a large, slab sided turret which was cramped for the crew, had limited traverse and limited elevation. Fortunately by the time Bishop was issued, 25-pdrs were no longer being called upon to act as AT guns, so it did not have a direct confrontation with any panzers, which is just as well.

The great improvement in the artillery support for tanks came with the issue of the M7 Priest. This was a 105-mm howitzer mounted on a modified Sherman hull. They were issued to one of the three artillery regiments of armoured divisions, and the 1st Armoured Division got them in time for Alamein. However although they were good, the need for them was less pronounced because the tanks were now Shermans able to fire their own High Explosive ammunition and capable of semi-indirect techniques.

The 105-mm gun of the Priests had a slightly longer range than the 25-pdr and fired a heavier shell, and its accurate airburst fuze and its flashless propellant made it many friends, but the longer range was not that important when providing close support for tanks and the 25-pdr's capacity for providing a sustained high rate of fire made it a generally more useful gun. The high rate of fire was possible because of the gun shield. This was not there, as with the 2-pdr, to protect the crew from shrapnel and SA fire, but to protect them from the blast of the gun's own rounds. Without this protection the crew would soon wilt.

The artillery regiment associated with 2nd Armoured Brigade was 11th (HAC) regiment, RHA. The Honourable Artillery Company was a normal territorial regiment but can be regarded as almost a holding unit for potential officers. The positive result of this was that the regiment was composed of high quality personnel, the unfortunate result was that there was a high turnover of personnel, particularly early in the war when there was a dire shortage of officers.

Artillery regiments made up of the HAC and some of the yeomanry regiments were given the RHA title, almost as a social courtesy.

A field or horse artillery regiment contained three eight-gun batteries. In England the batteries of the 11th RHA were attached one to each of the armoured regiments of 2nd Armoured Brigade, as were companies of the 9th Battalion, RB. This organisation remained in force until the brigade deployed at Sauna when both the artillery and infantry were withdrawn from the brigade to join the support group. Once there they were organised into battery-company 'Jock' columns and sent to harass the Germans in the area to the south of El Agheila.

This deployment might have worked if the Germans had been content to be harassed, but they had been underrated and, on 21st January 1942, they attacked in full strength. The result was a disaster. 'A' battery lost all its guns, 'B' lost two and 'E' lost three. About half of the lost guns were abandoned when they bogged down in soft sand. Also the regiment lost at least 54 vehicles and 70 men. The three columns finally rejoined the division on the Gazala Line where the batteries were returned to their previous armoured regiments and in that organisation the regiment fought through the Gazala battle until heavy casualties both among guns and tanks made that organisation unrecognisable. An AT battery was attached to the regiment just before the battle started, and it stayed throughout the battle despite heavy casualties.

Attaching batteries of AT guns to RHA regiments was to become standard practice as AT regiments were broken up, a process started in may 1942. At the same time a start was made replacing 2-pdrs with 6-pdrs.

After the Gazala battle the survivors formed a composite battery which supported South African and New Zealand troops on the Alamein line. During the Gazala battle and the retreat to Alamein the regiment lost 63 officers and men killed, 177 wounded and 211 captured, out of an establishment of approximately 580. Of those taken prisoner, 53 died when the ship carrying them to Italy was torpedoed and sunk. As the situation stabilised the regiment was withdrawn to absorb reinforcements and train on 'Priests'. It was the first British regiment to be issued with these self-propelled guns.

The regiment rejoined 2nd Armoured Brigade, the batteries attached to the same regiments and with them went through the Battle of Alamein, being stuck in the minefields with the tanks, but at least the armour of the priests was a protection for the gun detachments.

In Tunisia 11th RHA was moved to 6th Armoured Division, then went to Sicily but rejoined 1st Armoured Division in North Africa.

The smooth cooperation between artillery and armour which

obtained in 2nd Armoured Brigade was not repeated in 22nd Armoured Brigade. The organisation was the same, with a battery of 107th (South Notts Hussars) regiment RHA, two troops from an AT regiment and a company from 50th Reconnaissance Regiment, which had recently been 4th Northumberland Fusiliers, attached to each armoured regiment but the concept was different. In 2nd Armoured Brigade the idea was for the artillery to follow the tanks and with indirect fire to increase the armoured regiment's firepower. In 22nd Armoured Brigade the idea was for the guns and infantry to form a static box for the tanks to manoeuvre around, and that was roughly what happened in action. There was also a plan for, in an advance when a clash with German armour was expected, the artillery and infantry box to go before the tanks to give the Germans something to attack so that the tanks could take them in the flank. This was not tried in action.

The 22nd Armoured Brigade was first in action with its new organisation on the first day of the Battle of Gazala, 27th May 1942. It was posted close to, and on the south of, the Knightsbridge box. The three armoured regiments forming a line running south, 3rd CLY by Knightsbridge, then 4th CLY and 2nd RGH in the south. Two days earlier the RGH had been moved to the south a short distance but the move was only to be temporary and the vehicles and guns were not dug in.

The Germans caught 22nd Armoured Brigade entirely by surprise. The RGH box quickly lost its battery commander who went out in an AOP armoured car to investigate the situation, and the German tanks were soon able to engage the guns, half of which were destroyed before the survivors were ordered to fall back on the rest of the brigade. Once the surviving guns joined the other two boxes all the guns formed a line on a ridge running to the north-west from the Knightsbridge box, and they stayed there throughout that part of the battle. The RGH had taken very heavy casualties, but the two CLY regiments successfully engaged the Germans, covered by the fire of their supporting guns.

The next operation 22nd Armoured Brigade was involved in was to see the destruction of the regimental boxes, this was the assault of the 'Cauldron'. The armoured brigade was to drive into the cauldron after an infantry division had breached its defences. The operation was disastrous primarily because the Germans were underestimated. It was believed that they were beaten and in the process of withdrawing, but the opposite was true. The brigade came under heavy fire from front and both sides which halted it. In the evening the tanks withdrew but the guns and infantry were ordered to stay in place. This they did and were effectively abandoned. Next day the Germans closed in on them and the artillery regiment and infantry battalion were wiped out.

Notes

1 'Army Training Instruction No 3, Handling of an Armoured Division'

2 'Operation Desert Sabre', Army Code 71520

3 'The Tactical Handling of the Armoured Division and its components, Part 3, The Motor Battalion', June 1943. This manual is now rare and these quotes come from 'British and Commonwealth Motorized Infantry Tactics in WWII', the Nafziger Collection, 2011, which is an American copy of the British manual. American spelling and 'typos' have been corrected.

Chapter 13
Attacking the Gothic Line

In August 1944 the Italian campaign seemed to be reaching a climax, there was just one German defensive position, the Gothic Line, left before a triumphal surge possibly as far as Venice, or even Vienna. However events were to prove this optimism to be wildly delusional.

The major part of the 8th Army offensive was to be carried by V Corps which General Leese called his 'pursuit corps', and the fundamentals of the corps plan would have seemed like common sense. The German front was to be breached by two infantry divisions, 46th and 56th, then 1st Armoured Division would breakout through the gap they had made to the Romagna plain.

The battle turned out to be much harder than expected and broke down into three phases, almost three different battles from the point of view of 1st Armoured Division. The climax of each phase saw an attempted breakthrough by the division. All of them failed. The division did not do very well in this battle. The Official History refers to it as 'untrained' and an '*ad-hoc* last minute grouping of three brigades'. It had had no experience of operating in mountainous country and General Hull only took over command on 14th August. In view of the manpower shortage afflicting 8th Army it is not surprising that the division was to be disbanded after the close of the Gothic Line fighting.

V Corps
Commander Lieutenant General C Keightley
    7th Armoured Brigade
    25th Tank Brigade
    1st Armoured Division, Major General Hull
        4th Hussars
        2nd Armoured Brigade, Brigadier Goodbody
            Queens Bays
            9th Lancers

        10th Hussars
        1st KRRC (Motor battalion)
        18th (lorried) Infantry Brigade
        43rd Infantry Brigade (Gurkhas)
4th Infantry Division
46th Infantry Division
56th Infantry Division
4th Indian Infantry Division

The Defences

The Gothic Line can be taken as the area between the rivers Foglia and Marecchia. The rivers were approximately 20 miles apart. There was a lightly defended forward zone between the Foglia and the Metauno, this was about 12 miles deep but of no significance to the armoured division. *(See Sketch 6)*

The main defended zone comprised of difficult country. It was hilly and the roads, which ran along valleys, were few, narrow and easily blocked, particularly by mud. The River Marano was to prove a major obstacle. The weather was to be wet throughout most of the operation and the area was intersected by many streams that would quickly become significant obstacles in the rain, most bridges being down.

The German garrison was confident of holding the Allies off until autumn by which time the weather would have been so bad that their progress would have been halted till spring. However their task was not made easier by the paucity of armour available to them. This gave them limited scope for major counter-attacks. No doubt the extensive demolition of bridges was carried out because the Germans knew there would be few counter-attacks. German defensive tactics relied on counter-attacks, but in the absence of armour, infantry-based counter-attacks could result in attrition that would work against the defenders.

Probably the greatest strength of the Gothic Line was in the minds of the allies in that they grossly underestimated the problems it would cause. It was assumed that an assault would just crash through it and the lesson of the western front during the Great War, that an attack should progress methodically from one high point to the next, was ignored. The high ground provided observation posts for the artillery, and the battle on the Gothic Line was to be dominated by artillery as most modern battles have been.

The Course of the Battle, Phase 1
On 25th August 1944 the operation started with the crossing of the Metauno, and on 29th August the 46th Division was on the banks of the Folgia facing the Gothic Line. Next day leading troops of the division crossed the river. German tactics in Italy for the defence of rivers were not to defend the river's edge but to dig in further back on high ground and catch the attackers in a killing zone. The German defence of the Folgia seems not to have been up to their usual standard, giving some credence to the concept that the Gothic Line was undermanned and would not be much of an obstacle.

The infantry divisions fought their way forward and by 3rd September everything seemed to be going well. General Alexander was to write: 'It had been a great success for Eighth Army. By a combination of surprise in preparation and dash in the attack, they had swept through a fortified line which had been twelve months in preparation almost as though it were not there.' However there were two things that should have caused some unease.

To the east of the British front the Canadian corps was making good progress, but an attack on the high ground of Point 204 proved disastrous. The position was to be carried by an infantry battalion and a Sherman regiment. Artillery fire halted the infantry and the tanks went on without them. They were easy targets on the bare hillsides for a battery of 88s and the regiment was effectively wiped out. Clearly armour had to be used carefully, particularly so as the Germans were moving up significant reinforcements.

The limit of the prepared positions of the Gothic Line was initially taken to be the river Marano. If the infantry could capture a crossing over this river then the 1st Armoured Division would be able to surge through and the back of the campaign would be broken. Unfortunately the plan fell apart due to a general over-confidence. The 46th Division did not reach the Marano. Their advanced units got close to it but the weight of German artillery halted them. They were badly overlooked, particularly from the Gemmano and Coriano ridges to their left and rear.

The move forward for the tanks was not an easy one, even getting to the Metauro involved a long and difficult drive but the crews had only two hours rest then they had to move, just after midnight on the morning of 3rd September en route to their laager on the south bank of the Folgia. The 2nd Armoured Brigade arrived around 8.00 am. The march had been nearly continuous for 50 hours and its control had not been helped by the brigade HQ's armoured command vehicle tipping over with the brigadier and brigade-major, the principal staff officer, in it.

The brigade had lost 20 tanks due to mechanical failure, though some had just run out of petrol due to heavy going, and some of these tanks would rejoin their units later. However the brigade had been fortunate in one respect in that, shortly before the start of this operation, the brigade's armoured regimental fitters had been issued with half-tracks, replacing their lorries. This helped the fitters to keep up with the tanks in the bad going.

The armoured brigade now had a break to carry out maintenance and sleep, but the divisional reconnaissance regiment, 4th Hussars, was, at first light, already probing towards the river Conca to locate crossings. Unfortunately this probing must have been done with a little too much drive as the leading squadron, moving across country, drove into a marsh and the whole squadron bogged down, as did the following squadron. Consequently the colonel, sending forward the remaining sabre squadron, gave it strict orders to keep to the roads. It did this, but found its way barred by a deep and fast-flowing stream. There was a bridge but it was badly damaged and did not look as if it could carry a tank, unfortunately the road the squadron was on was so narrow as to prevent the tanks turning round so the squadron had to try the bridge. Half the squadron made it, then the bridge collapsed.

The half squadron that did not make it had to struggle backwards, then it set off on a different route and finally joined up with the leading half squadron, which had found the front line on a ridge overlooking the Conca. As radios did not work well in broken country, and as a guide would be required, an NCO in a sawn-off Honey was sent back to the Colonel who was waiting with the two squadrons that had now been freed from the mud. He arrived around dark and the regiment made its way forward along the difficult path the second half squadron had taken, led by the NCO from that squadron. Unfortunately as night descended he got lost.

The colonel halted the regiment, as wandering around the hills at night would not have been that sensible. Then the officers opened some bottles of wine, there not being that much else to do. Fortunately though, some were alert and heard tank engines in the distance. The regiment drove in the direction of the noise and found the advanced squadron. No doubt the relief was mutual.

At first light the regiment crept down to the Conca. Some infantry had crossed and were working their way forward and the Hussars provided some fire support, but as the rest of the armoured division was on its way the Hussars were ordered to pull off the road and let it pass. They found a field and stayed in it all day, coming under sporadic mortar fire. In the late afternoon the motor battalion came up and took over from them, so they withdrew. It would appear that the close country of the Gothic Line did not offer an environment in which an armoured reconnaissance regiment could show its form.

The three armoured regiments of 2nd Armoured Brigade had crossed the Foglia on 3rd September and spent the night just north of the river. At 8.00 pm at an 'O' group the brigadier was instructed to cross the Conca as soon as possible, then his brigade would cover the deployment of the rest of the division as it prepared to pass through the 46th Division, the first phase of the breakout.

Remarkably when these orders were given it was not known if 46th Division had reached the Marano, which had been rather arbitrarily chosen as the northern boundary of the Gothic Line. Whether it was or not was also not known. The division's reconnaissance regiment was nowhere near the Marano, but its reports could not have been optimistic. Nevertheless the brigadier decided to move forward overnight to capture San Savino at first light, 4th September. This would secure a large area for the division to form up in, and was handy to move forward from as soon as the infantry secured a bridgehead across the Marano.

The order of march was 10th Hussars, motor battalion, some self-propelled guns, Bays and 9th Lancers. Unfortunately, but possibly predictably, the march was chaos. The move started at 1.30am and at 8.0 the leading regiment arrived at the Conca and found that the ford it was to use was blocked by some wheeled vehicles of Divisional HQ, the crews of which were drinking tea and listening to records. The Hussars' colonel sorted that out. The Hussars moved forward about a mile but found that they were behind some Canadian tanks which were supporting some infantry, this action being only 4,000 yards north of the Conca.

Plainly there was no gap for the tanks to pour through so General Hull decided to make his own gap as soon as possible. His first move would be to assault San Savino from the 46th Division's position at San Clemente. Then he would progress via Vecciano to the Marano. The armoured brigade was to advance with 10th Hussars on the right, the Bays on the left, each supported by a company of the motor battalion. The remainder of the motor battalion and the 9th Lancers would be in reserve. The artillery support would be impressive.

Unfortunately the original start line was unsuitable either still being occupied by the Germans or covered by their fire, so it was moved back. Even so the Bays had a great deal of difficulty in getting to it. On the left 'C' squadron, moving along the north bank of the Conca under AT gunfire from Gemmano and Croce lost four tanks, then, as it approached Coriano and the start line, a tank was knocked out by a panzerfaust. Just as the squadron reached the start line the squadron leader and his 2 i/c took the wrong turn and ran into some Germans. They knocked out a panzer, but soon both their tanks were hit. The commanders and crews baled out and after various adventures managed to rejoin their regiment a few days later. This, though, did remove the squadron's command element from the battle.

The colonel of the Bays, observing that one of his squadrons was now at less than half strength and without its commander, ordered 'A' squadron, on the right, to extend the left, there not being time to bring up 'B' squadron from reserve. Unfortunately on the loose earth of the hillside this move caused some 'A' squadron tanks to lose their tracks.

Finally, at 4.35pm 4th September, 50 minutes late, the advance started, but was halted after three quarters of a mile due to heavy fire and casualties. The Bays were now understrength, the brigade's tank strength was:

    Bays,   19 Shermans, 11 Stuarts
    Lancers   32   9
    Hussars   30   10
    Brigade HQ   5

The 9th Lancers were ordered up believing that the leading regiments were on the objective and they were surprised to see many tanks of the leading regiments still around and before the start line, no doubt in most cases the crews were 'track bashing'. The Lancers were ordered in the direction of San Savino but the same problem occurred. As soon as they came under fire the commanders closed down and as the ground was very rough and broken the drivers made mistakes. Two of the Lancers' tanks overturned in a gully, and some bogged down, the ground being soft with rain. The three regiments fell back to the San Clemente to Cevolabbate road which was their original start line. Presently an infantry battalion came up and relieved them. The three armoured regiments, Bays, Lancers and Hussars were left with tank strengths of 21, 30 and 30 Shermans.

Next morning, 5th September, it was decided to try again, this time with a single squadron of Lancers. They were to be supported by fire from the other two squadrons of the regiment which had formed up close to Cevolabbate. The assaulting squadron was to have been supported by the motor battalion, but when the infantry had not turned up by 9.00 am, an hour after the squadron should have jumped off, it went without them. This time the squadron only lost two tanks bogged down, but as the Lancers approached San Savino they were held up by panzerfaust men, and two tanks were knocked out by a German tank. The Lancers seem to have reached an impasse but fortunately a platoon of the motor battalion arrived, they must have run 8,000 yards to get there, and they started clearing the panzerfaust men back to allow the tanks forward to take firm possession a cemetery on the southern side of the village. In the Italian campaign it was remarkable how much fighting there was in and around cemeteries, probably because of the thick walls and ground that was easy to dig into.

Clearly a weak squadron of tanks and an infantry platoon could not capture the whole village, but the Germans, who were trying to counter-attack were held at bay by the fire of six field artillery regiments. By last light an infantry battalion, 1st Buffs, came up, it was not the motor battalion but from one of the lorried brigades. *En route* this battalion was fired on by 56th Division and was caught in a British artillery barrage. The Lancers pulled back carrying the Buffs casualties on their tanks. The other two battalions of the brigade came up and overnight put in an attack on San Savino. It was not a total success and they dug in on the outskirts. Then it started to rain heavily.

The brigade commander had gone forward to watch this action, and his place in the command tank was taken by his second-in-command, Colonel Macdonell. Command tanks had their main armaments removed to free up space in their turrets. To disguise the tanks' employment the gun barrels were replaced by wooden poles. The command tank was targeted by German artillery and a round struck the front of the tank, driving the imitation barrel back into the turret, killing Colonel Macdonell. Until shortly before his death, Colonel Macdonell had commanded the 9th Lancers.

During the day the 10th Hussars, which had been in reserve, had sent the reconnaissance troop to make contact with the 4th Hussars. In doing so this troop located some Germans and the regiment decided to practice its indirect fire skills. It was not a success. The trajectory of the 75mm was too flat to clear the crests. It did, though, provoke a German response in the form of an artillery salvo which hit an 'O' group, killing two and wounding several others.

After the failure at San Savino the army commander decided to accept the inevitable and called a halt. Whereas the accent so far had been on speed, from now on there would be a more deliberate approach.

There is no doubt that seen as an attempted breakthrough this action so far was a failure and the cause was a breakdown of communications. When the tanks were ordered forward the infantry were not sure where their troops were but believed that they were on the Marano. The 4th Hussars, who must have known better, were not believed. Had a more 'set piece' approach to the battle been taken, and the attack advanced from one ridge or hill to the next, then it might, or might not, have advanced more slowly but radios would have worked better and this kind of communications breakdown would have been less likely.

The Course of the Battle, Phase 2
This phase was mostly undertaken during heavy rain which reduced roads to almost bottomless mud and streams to raging torrents. It also reduced the effectiveness of air support. The Canadian Corps on the right of V Corps was now well ahead, so V Corps was given the task of capturing the strong German positions on high ground to protect the Canadian left. The heaviest fighting occurred at Gemmano, but naturally the San Savino-Coriano ridge was high priority.

By 6th September, when the armoured assault had ground to a halt, both infantry brigades of the division were across the Conca and the attack now became an infantry operation. The 43rd (Gurkha) Brigade was on the right, by San Clemente, and 18th Brigade was on the left, facing the Coriano Ridge. Coriano, the village after which the ridge was named, was on the right and was to be attacked by the Canadians.

A squadron of the 10th Hussars was attached to 18th Brigade to relieve the Lancers for a few days before the assault on the ridge. The deployment of the Gurkhas had a tragic result. A Hussar officer, making is way on foot to visit the detached squadron, was challenged by a Gurkha sentry. The sentry, of course, was not speaking English and the officer, assuming the language was German, opened fire. The sentry killed him.

To coincide with an attack by 56th Division on the left, the 18th Brigade put in an attack over night on San Savino, which was partly successful but in the morning a counter-attack drove it back. The next assault was to be mounted at night by elements of both brigades. The 43rd Brigade, supported by the Bays, was to attack due west, its objective being the crest of the ridge from Passano on the right to, but not including, San Savino on the left. The 18th Brigade, supported by the 9th Lancers, was to capture San Savino. Once the ridge was secure, 2nd Armoured Brigade was to surge through at least as far as the Marano. As the most difficult task had been allotted to the Bays, and as that regiment was short of tanks, it was given five Shermans by the Hussars and four by the Lancers.

The task was clearly a formidable one. The Gurkhas were to attack with two battalions forward, a squadron of the Bays supporting each. To ensure that the inevitable counter-attack next morning did not drive the Gurkhas back the tanks were to tow the Gurkhas' 6-pdrs onto the ridge to have them in place by dawn.

A study of the ground to be covered showed a wadi at the base of the ridge. It was passable on the left, where 'C' squadron was to attack, but on the right it was not, and the bridge was down. This problem was to be overcome by the use of an 'Ark'. This was a specialised form of armour which, in effect, was a Churchill tank without its turret, with ramps at each end and a tread way across the top. It was to be driven into the wadi to provide a temporary bridge.

The attack was postponed for a day to coincide with a Canadian operation, and then until 12th September to co-ordinate with 5th Army. The Bays used this delay to practice towing 6-pdrs. The 10th Hussars, who were now back in reserve, were to provide fire support and spent the last day ranging in on their targets. In the event the regiment fired 840 rounds in its artillery role.

At 5.00 pm on 12th September 'B' and 'C' squadrons of the Bays set off to link up with their battalions. The regimental HQ joined the brigade HQ. The artillery barrage started at 6.0 pm, and lasted till 11.00 pm. At 10.0 pm the two squadrons started forward in single file along narrow tracks, the tanks towing the AT guns with the gun crews riding on the tanks. The tanks were escorted by some Bren gun carriers. The march was as difficult as some night marches in the desert because of the dust thrown up by the tanks. On the left, 'C' squadron did well. The wadi crossing points were covered by German fire, and several tanks became ditched, but enough kept up with their infantry to deliver the AT guns and provide the firepower required.

Things did not work out as well on the right, 'B' squadron had further to go, and its radio link with the battalion it was supporting was not working, but as it approached the wadi it found out, from the FOO, that the Ark was not in place. Consequently the squadron leader decided to swing to the left and use one of the 'C' squadron crossings. This manoeuvre was not that easy because of the 6-pdrs being towed. The gun crews could not be called on to dismount, and uncouple the guns while the tanks turned. This would be extremely difficult to do at night and the leading tank had already come under artillery or mortar fire which destroyed the gun and wiped out its crew. The leading two troops found a field they could drive round in, the other tanks backed up. The situation was made worse when the squadron leader's tank tipped over in a roadside ditch. With these difficulties it is not surprising that the wadi was crossed only just before dawn. The squadron was then behind the wrong battalion so it had to drive quickly to the right one. It lost two tanks on mines, but arrived in time to help repulse the counter-attack which was just getting started.

Both squadrons were then in good hull-down positions. For a short while they came under AT gunfire from Coriano, but soon the Canadians stopped that and 'A' squadron came up behind the other two and it looked as if the pursuit was soon to start. However the 18th Brigade was having trouble in San Savino and the Lancers could not start from there until after 4.00 pm. When they did they got onto the Ripa Bianca ridge, but did not go very far being slowed by mines and AT guns, and then came to the Rio delle Formali which had, in the rain, grown from a trivial stream to become a considerable obstacle. The Lancers slowed to a halt and the KRRC was sent forward to take over from the tanks. Engineers bridged this stream overnight with an Ark, but too late to get the tanks across. The Bays pulled back a few hundred yards from the ridge, and settled down for the night.

The 1st Armoured Division could feel that it had achieved a great deal that day. It had captured a strong position and nearly 800 prisoners, but it had not achieved a breakthrough. The 9th Lancers stayed with 18th Brigade, making but slow progress.

The Course of the Battle, Phase 3
The recurring theme was that the Gothic Line was always that bit deeper than expected, and there was no alternative to slogging on through it. Overnight infantry of 56th Division established themselves on high ground along the Marano and the 4th Infantry Division moved up prior to crossing the river. The plan was now for the Gurkhas, as soon as possible, to cross the Marano between the two bridgeheads, then for 2nd Armoured Brigade to breakout through their bridgehead.

On 15th September the 10th Hussars took over from the Lancers on the Ripa Bianca ridge and linked up with the Gurkhas. Unfortunately the infantry were held up by artillery and mortar fire as they moved forward along the muddy roads, and when they arrived at their assembly area they were heavily shelled. Consequently the assault was delayed until the next morning. The crossing was successful, closely supported by the Hussars who crossed the river on the 17th.

As the 1st Armoured Division closed up to, and crossed the Marano it could plainly see the Ceriano-San Fortunato ridge. This was a part of the Rimini Line which was now confidently believed to be the last position on the Gothic Line. Beyond that was the small stream of the Marecchia, then the Romagna plain. In front of the Rimini Line ran the shallow Ausa river.

The leading troops of the 56th Division crossed the Ausa on 18th September. To the right the 1st Armoured Division kept up, but to the right of the armoured division, 4th Division was lagging, held up at Aquilina. It had found that it had to attack Cerasolo on its left because it gave the Germans such excellent artillery observation. Cerasolo should have been an objective for the 1st Armoured Division because this had the effect of restricting the front 1st Armoured Division could deploy across. Even so everything seemed set for the last push. Time for this was running out, the weather was on the verge of breaking. Up to this point the rain had caused immense problems, but they would be nothing compared to the problems to come. Everyone, particularly 2nd Armoured

Brigade, was aware of the need for speed.

As the leading troops of the 2nd Armoured Brigade reached the Ausa the brigade was given the task of capturing an area of high ground called Point 153. This was the eastern limit of the Ceriano Ridge and dominated the area, after that the objective was the Marecchio. No time scale was given, other than that it should be done as soon as possible.

The initial plan was to cross the Ausa and to advance on a two regimental front, the Bays group on the left and the Lancers on the right. Each regimental group was to include an artillery battery, an infantry company and a Valentine bridgelayer. A two regimental deployment may have been possible when crossing the ridge and exploiting to the north, but not on the way there. There was only one practical route. The brigade had to swing to the left to use the main Rimini-San Marino road, the Bays leading. There was a further problem in that the route was badly overlooked from the west. To overcome this the brigade was to take advantage of the advance of the 7th Armoured Brigade, on Churchills, supporting 56th Division. In the wake of this brigade the Yorkshire Dragoons, with 'A' squadron of the Bays, was to occupy Point 146 to the left of the main route. This to be done before the brigade moved off. Also the KRRC, less the two companies with the Bays and Lancers, was to advance behind the 7th Armoured Brigade and occupy the crossroads around 2,000 yards to the west of Point 153.

It was considered that with the crossroads occupied and the Canadians on San Fortunato to the right, the Bays should easily be on Point 153. The Lancers would follow the Bays to cope with contingencies.

There were three things wrong with this plan, even if it was the best available under the circumstances. One was that the motor battalion was given too much to do, so the assaulting tanks would not have enough infantry support. Secondly there was little time for reconnaissance. Finally when the plan was decided upon the bulk of the armoured brigade was still to the south of the Marano and making slow progress in interminable traffic jams.

The order was issued at 7.30 pm on 18th September to the two regimental groups for an overnight move. It was cancelled later, but 'A' squadron of the Bays, did go and with the Dragoons occupied Point 146. They were driven off but counter-attacked and were firmly in possession at dawn, 5.30 am. An infantry battalion from 18th Brigade formed a bridgehead across the Ausa. The rest of the Bays started off at dawn and crossed the Marano at 8.00 am, then dispersed, under the cover of some trees, awaiting news of the progress of 7th Armoured Brigade.

At 8.30 a report was received that 7th Armoured Brigade was making progress along the Rimini road. At 9.00 am the Brigadier visited the Colonel of the Bays, then nothing else was heard until 2.20 pm when the Bays received an order from brigade to the effect that, as the rest of the corps was making excellent progress, the brigade would advance to seize Point 153 at first light next morning.

At 3.05 pm another order was received ordering the Bays group to advance immediately. This gave about four hours of daylight. As the Ausa was three and a half miles away it can be seen that it was a very tight schedule just to get to Point 153, let alone fight to get there.

The regiment crossed the Ausa at 4.45 pm and progressed westwards along the main road. When the column turned north off the Rimini road it passed 'A' squadron at Point 146. This squadron rejoined the regiment towards the rear of the regimental column even though it was short of fuel and ammunition and there was no real chance of getting the echelon forward. The plan was to reach the crossroads then, taking one of the roads as the start line, attack Point 153. However the road up to the crossroads crossed several spurs, and this slowed the column down so the Colonel of the Bays decided to put off the attack until the next morning, or as he might have put it, to stick to the 2.20 am orders.

Progress was also slow crossing the Ausa where, at 11.00 pm, one of the Lancers' tanks bogged down, which held up traffic for an hour.

Overnight a patrol from the motor battalion was sent forward to Point 153 and it was found to be occupied. At 3.30am on the 20th the Bays received an order to attack at first light supported by 'A' squadron of 9th Lancers. They moved up to the start line but they were tightly boxed in by steep ground and the move was, as usual, difficult despite the provision of artificial moonlight produced by the shining of searchlights on clouds. As they arrived a Honey from Recce Troop was knocked out by a panzerfaust and German infantrymen were reported to be active, so a platoon of the motor battalion was sent up to clear the area. Worse than this, they found that they were receiving fire from high ground to the left. This ground had been cleared by 7th Armoured Brigade but, because there were few infantry to secure it, German troops had infiltrated back into it and driven the British infantry off.

The Colonel decided to send a troop of tanks from 'B' squadron on the left to clear this high ground, but as these tanks left the shelter of their hull-down position all three were knocked out by AT guns firing from close to Point 153. The tanks could not pin point the guns, and if a tank commander tried to study the ground through binoculars, he came under heavy small arms fire from the high ground to the left. Another squadron of the Lancers, 'B' squadron, was put under command of the Bays.

The stage was now set for two squadrons of the Bays to charge Point 153, across around 2,000 yards of absolutely open country. The assault was to be made by 'B' and 'C' squadrons with 'C' squadron, on the right, leading; 'B' squadron, on the left, had only four tanks left in its sabre troops. 'A' squadron, which was now short of fuel and ammunition, was to give fire support, but, obviously, could not give much. It seems that the Brigadier was unhappy with the order, the Colonel, with a proper British understatement had, to quote the regimental war diary, said that *'he didn't think it would be much of a show.'* Unfortunately with the congestion on the roads being so bad the Brigadier could not get back to divisional HQ to present his point of view and he did not want to list his misgivings in clear on the radio, though it is not obvious why he could not have used code. Regardless of the Brigadier's objections the senior command at corps and division was determined that the breakthrough was imminent and all that was needed was one determined charge by the tanks. The order came back at 9.45am that the Bays should attack in 15 minutes. The tanks did not actually charge till 11.50am, having waited to allow 9th Lancers to move up.

The charge became a massacre, nearly all the tanks were knocked out, mostly by a battery of AT guns behind the high ground to the left. Three 'B' squadron tanks made it back, none from 'C' squadron. At least one 'C' Squadron tank nearly reached the objective, from which the crews would have been able to lookdown on the Romagna plain. A troop leader was heard on the radio to say *'I can see the plain. I can see the plain.'* Then silence.

The 9th Lancers should have followed the Bays, but after further representations by the Brigadier the orders were changed and the attack called off. As the brigade war diary entry for 12.20pm had it:

'9L reported it was impossible to make any headway, it was like "butting one's head against a brick wall". Every time a BAYS tank had crossed the ridge it had been picked off. The houses at the Start Pt were still held by enemy inf. Who were able to machine gun crews at very short range as they baled out. It would be advisable to form a new plan of attack'.

The 14th Foresters, from 18th Brigade, took over from the tanks and KRRC, and the Lancers left two troops in support. The rest of the 2nd Armoured Brigade assembled by the Ausa. Then the rain started and within 10 minutes all the tanks were bogged.

During the night the Germans, reacting to Canadian pressure on the right, started to fall back and towards dusk on 20th September explosions were heard as the Germans destroyed their stores. At what may be called the tipping point of the battle, 2nd Armoured Brigade tank strengths were:

```
Bays,     18 Shermans,  7 Stuarts
Lancers,  39            10
Hussars,  40            10
```

The German defence started to weaken, and 3rd Brigade was on Point 153 the following afternoon. Next day the 10th Hussars were placed under the command of 43rd Brigade for an attack, that night, across the Marecchia. This was to prove an ambitious undertaking. The operation started after dark. The Gurkhas were to advance with two battalions forward, a squadron of tanks supporting each battalion. They had 8,000 yards to cross to reach the river which was wide and shallow, then the brigade was to swing to the right to capture some low hills that ran southwards from Santarcangelo. Because of the distance, river and timescale it was very unlikely the Gurkhas' 6-pdrs could get forward so it was very important to have the tanks up on the final objective by dawn. However the main worry for the tanks was the river. Although it was shallow, crossing places had to be carefully reconnoitred to prevent tanks falling into deep pools, striking mines or hitting other hazards.

The Gurkhas reached and crossed the river easily enough but once on the far side, as was so often the case in Italy, they came under heavy fire and could make no further progress. The tanks arrived at the river to find no crossings marked, so this task had to be undertaken by the Reconnaissance Troop in its sawn-off Honeys – usually called 'Runnies' by the Hussars. By the time that the tanks were across the Gurkhas had moved forward and the tanks made what speed they could, covering 1,200 yards before they were held up by a deep drainage ditch, so much a feature of this part of Italy. The only bridge was, predictably, down, but the Reconnaissance Troop once again showed its form and constructed a crossing with railway sleepers. By this time the sun was up and the tanks arrived at the infantry's position just in time. The Germans had registered the location for their artillery and soon blasted the Gurkhas off the hills. The two battalions fell back and the tanks were left holding the line by themselves. In the afternoon the reserve Gurkha battalion came up and re-occupied the position, but Germans artillery and mortar fire remained heavy all day.

Next day the German fire started to weaken and the Gurkhas occupied Santarcangelo. The tanks were withdrawn the next day, and the following day, 26th September, 2nd Armoured Brigade was placed under the orders of 46th Division. It had been announced on 22nd September that the 1st Armoured Division was to be disbanded, and now it ceased to exist, though the divisional HQ continued to function for a short time to control 18th Brigade and two ad-hoc groups, Wheeler Force and Elbo Force, which were holding the line to screen the assembly of the Polish Corps. Then it too ceased to exist.

Chapter 14
Disbandment

In view of the manpower shortage obtaining in Italy as troops were transferred to North-West Europe and casualties ate into fighting formations, it could have come as little surprise that some formations were selected for disbandment.

As the Official History put it:

'On 22nd September Alexander accepted his staff's proposal that all infantry battalions should be reduced from four to three rifle companies, with a drop in established strength from 36 officers and 809 men to 30 officers and 700 men; that two infantry brigades should be reduced to cadre; and that 1st Armoured Division should be broken up into its constituent parts which would be used to reinforce other formations.'

At the time it must have been assumed that 1st Armoured Division was selected to be broken up as a result of its poor performance on the Gothic Line, but this is not the fact. General Alexander, the Commander-in-Chief, Allied Army Italy, had decided, in a memo dated 8th June 1944 [1], that the division should be disbanded. A copy of this memo is reproduced in Appendix 4.

Reaction to the news of the division's end is best conveyed by quoting a section of 9th Lancers' war diary:

'It is only to be expected that the end of the First Armoured Division is a great disappointment. It was the original and only Regular Armoured Division in the British Army, possessing great and enviable tradition which all ranks have done so much to win. During recent months, however, the Staff have completely changed and no one has any confidence in them. This has caused a marked defect in the recent fighting of the Division as a whole. Furthermore, of the three Brigades the Second Armoured Brigade is the only

one that has been with the division from start to finish; it has, in fact, been the Division. 18 lorried Infantry Brigade joined but a year ago, and 43 G.L.B. only a month ago; and so the White Rhino is handed down to the Second Armoured Brigade as their sign – to whom he rightfully belongs.'

Its poor performance on the Gothic Line was not held against its commander and Major General Hull was given the command of 5th Infantry Division that was transferred to North West Europe. The 2nd Armoured Brigade continued its existence but as an independent brigade, under a different brigadier. The 18th (Lorried) Brigade was broken up and the Yorkshire Dragoons (9th KOYLI), which had had such a varied career, was placed in suspended animation to be reformed after the war.

Note 1

TNA WO 204/1291

Chapter 15
Conclusion

The previous chapters have given a brief history of the 1st Armoured Division. It cannot be denied that this division has, over the years, received a bad press, and that its activities during the retreat to Alamein showed the very worst aspects of British tank warfare. However, the division at its worst was showing the effects of seven months of near continuous action, which involved mostly defeat and retreat.

The final action, the assault of the Gothic Line, was disastrous but not more so than 7th Armoured Division's defeat at Villers-Bocage or 11th Armoured Division in Operation Goodwood, and yet both of these divisions have received a good press and there are several popular divisional histories, particularly of the 7th, in print. Comparisons are always invidious, but 1st Armoured Division's reputation can stand as high as any. In its defeat in January 1942 the division did not fall apart as 2nd Armoured Division did in similar circumstances in April the previous year and if, during the Ruweisat battles before Alamein, its reputation with some infantry units was poor, at least it did not dash itself to pieces on a *pakfront* as 23rd Armoured Brigade did.

There is currently no history of 1st Armoured Division in print, and the oblivion into which this division has been cast seems a little undeserved, consequently it is hoped that this account will go some small way to rectifying this.

Appendix 1

Many Arab place names include a description, some useful ones are:

Alam	cairn or rock
Bab	pass or gate
Bir	well or cistern
Deir	depression
(D)Jebel	mountain
Mersa	port
Naqb	pass or gate
Qaret	low hill
Sanyet	deep well.
Tel	hill, mound
Trig	track
Wadi	valley, usually dry.

Appendix 2

REPORT ON OPERATIONS IN THE LIBYAN DESERT
BY COMD
(TEMPORARY) 1 ARMD DIV.
21 JAN TO 4 FEB 1942

Part II - LESSONS

Training for Operations in the Desert

1. Every successful battle in the Middle East has been fought by troops specially trained and specially prepared for that battle over a long period. When we have been forced to throw in troops comparatively untrained in desert warfare, we have invariably suffered a reverse. Many officers who have become used to desert warfare do not realise that new troops have a great deal to learn before they can be really efficient. Everything is so really different to conditions in Europe – Driving, maintenance of vehicles, navigation, cooking, camouflage, sanitation, wireless operation are just a few of the daily tasks of a soldier which are quite different in the desert to Europe. Again our town bred soldiers have at first a fear of the desert, culled from American film scenes of vultures advancing slowly on a man dying of hunger and thirst; this has to be eradicated. Desert tactics, too, need special instruction. In my opinion it is necessary to give troops 3 months' training after arrival from Europe or any other non-desert country before they can be confidently thrown into battle in the desert.

Tactics

2. <u>Basis of operations</u>. All desert warfare is liable to be subject to ebb and flow, the spring and autumn tides being especially strong. It is very necessary therefore to build up strong breakwaters behind the flowing tide to stem the almost inevitable ebb. These defended areas should be systematically and thoroughly prepared behind our advance

as far forward as possible dependant on the administrative situation. Forward of these positions only light recce troops of the column type should be sent forward till the adm. Situation allows of the next bound forward by the main forces. Even then a sufficient garrison should be left to occupy the defences from behind which the further main advance is launched.

3. <u>Columns.</u> It is very necessary to realise the capacities and the limitations of our columns of all arms. They are excellent for recce, for counter-recce and for harassing, working in conjunction with armd cars in many cases. But they cannot fight a battle either in advance or in withdrawal. Careful thought must therefore be given to the number of columns really usefully employed. We are very apt to send out columns hither and thither which achieve little and which use up a large proportion of our guns, which are not then available or at any rate not fit and fresh for the main battle.

4. <u>Delay by Armoured Forces</u> Armoured forces cannot keep up a running fight in the withdrawal. The role of 'delay without becoming seriously engaged' sometimes allotted to them is an impractical one. The only method of imposing delay with armoured units is to put in a strong counter-attack and then withdrawal right back out of reach of any thrust by the enemy. An evening counter-attack is often the most suitable in withdrawal, recovery being carefully organised under cover of darkness and then a move back carried out in darkness beyond the range of a further thrust by the enemy on one petrol refill ie 40 miles.

5. <u>Formations of Armoured Forces</u>
I am convinced that Armoured Bdes should move and fight as concentrated as possible. Only such dispersion should be accepted as to permit of the protection of the guns, motorized infantry and 'A' echelon vehicles accompanying them. Otherwise the more compact the formation the better. Dispersion leads to loss of control and a disunited confused effort, concentration enables a hammer blow to be delivered at the right place and time under the close control of the

commander, every unit and arm acting in planned cooperation. For this form of combat a well thought out, carefully practiced battle array and battle drill is essential.

Appendix 3

STATEMENT BY MAJ-GEN. H. LUMSDEN
ACCOUNT OF OPERATIONS 1 ARMD DIV – 1 JULY 42.

1. EVENTS LEADING UP TO THE BATTLE
About mid-day 30 June, whilst withdrawing from the area SANYET GABRIYA 8131, 1 Armd Div was ordered to move East of the EL ALAMEIN Line coming into Eighth Army Reserve in the area 8928. The Div was to change from comd 13 Corps to comd 30 Corps on passing East of the EL ALAMEIN Line, although being in Eighth Army Reserve.

The bulk of the Div passed immediately North of the DEIR ES SHEIN box between 2000 and 2200 hrs 30 June after fighting and moving almost continuously for three days and three nights. At about 2200 hrs Div Recce parties reported the area 8928 to be a sea of sand and many vehicles already stuck. Requests were made for a better area to be allotted and Div HQ was told to try and find one as near to the allotted area as possible.

The only maps available were of a scale of 1:500,000 and in very small numbers, and in spite of many requests during the preceding 36 hrs, no accurate information as to own minefields, own wire or own tps had been received. Consequently at first light on 1 July the Div was disorganised, very many of the wheeled vehicles, particularly guns, were stuck in the sand and all tps and comds were dead tired.

2. EVENTS 1 JULY
The morning was spent locating tps of the Div and re-organising, towing vehicles out of the sand and trying to discover locations of neighbouring formations. At about 0600 hrs, a warning order for a withdrawal to the WADI NATRUN was received from 30 Corps (30 Corps O.O. No. 54 of 1Jul).

As at 1200 hrs no orders had been received for the task of the armour, 4 Armd Bde from area 891286 and 22 Armd Bde from area 425699 were moved on to and just south of the ridge in the area 889280.

Communications with 30 Corps were very bad. At 1325 hrs a message was sent to 30 Corps stating that their frequency for our rear link was so bad that we were unable to accept responsibility for the passage of information. No telephone line had been laid to the Div by either Corps.

Up to 1430 hrs the Div received no information of enemy movements from higher or flank formations, although our own Armd Cars had reported enemy movements Eastwards on the 292 and 288 Northings Grids.

At 1450 hrs 22 Armd Bde reported a large enemy column moving East along the 280 Northing Grid and at 1515 hrs 4 Armd Bde reported 38 tanks at 875281 moving SE with an additional 28 tanks further South. G.O.C. ordered 22 Armd Bde, whose strength in tanks on this day consisted of one weak composite regiment only, to move SW to the left of 4 Armd Bde and to attack the 28 enemy tanks reported in the South and prevent them penetrating our front or passing round our left flank.

At 1515 hrs a MOST IMMEDIATE Eighth Army message, T.O.O. 0925 hrs, was received placing 1 Armd Div under operational comd 30 Corps.

At 1610 hrs visibility was very bad owing to a sand-storm and the only tanks which could be seen were 8 moving in a South-westerly direction.

At 1625 hrs information was received from 30 Corps that there were 40 to 60 enemy tanks and lorried infantry overrunning the 18 Ind Inf Bde box at 876283. This was the first intimation that this box was being attacked by tanks or being overrun. In the 30 Corps Sitrep timed 0035 hrs 2 Jul it was stated that the NE corner of the box was attacked by 20 enemy tanks at 1245 hrs.

Although no specific action by 1 Armd Div was ordered, on receipt of this information that 18 Ind Inf Bde box was being attacked, the G.O.C. immediately ordered 4 and 22 Armd Bdes to move West and North to deal with these enemy tanks.

No sounds of firing or of a battle taking place were heard and great difficulty was experienced in locating and making contact with the enemy tanks.

At 1700 hrs 20 enemy tanks were reported at 873283 and 22 Armd Bde was therefore ordered to return from the South and to be prepared to concentrate with 4 Armd Bde.

Owing to the difficulty of working off the 1:500,000 map and of locating our own tps and the enemy accurately, it was not until 1900 hrs that 22 Armd Bde contacted the enemy tanks in the neighbourhood and South of the DEIR ES SHEIN Box, inflicting casualties and driving 15 off in a South-westerly direction. After this very successful action, 22 Armd Bde could see our own troops withdrawing from the box.

At 2025 hrs 22 Armd Bde counter-attacked enemy tanks who had passed round North of the box and were attacking them from the NE. This action lasted until 2100 hrs when 22 Armd Bde, whose sole tank Regt was the 4 C.L.Y., withdrew to leaguer.

This action halted the advance of the enemy tanks.

Appendix 4

Allied Forces Headquarters 8 June 44

1. The future of 1 Br Armd Div presents a difficult problem. Experience has shown conclusively that in this type of terrain an armd div requires two infantry brigades to balance the armoured component, and to maintain its momentum in enclosed country. For instance it frequently happens that the whole of an infantry brigade must be committed to drive in the enemy's outposts and to locate and pin his main line of resistance. If there is only one infantry brigade in the division a combined tank and infantry outflanking attack can only be carried out by detaching an infantry brigade from an infantry division, with consequent delay and dislocation, even if an infantry division with a brigade in reserve is within reach.

2. To provide armoured divisions with the additional infantry brigade required to put into effect the conclusion stated in the preceding paragraph the following measures have so far been taken:-

(a) 61 Inf Bde has been formed out of the motor battalions of 7,9 and 26 Armd Bdes and has been allocated to 6 Br Armd Div.
(b) 24 Gds Bde has been attached to 6 S.A. Armd Div.
(c) Comd 1 Cdn Corps has made urgent application to the Canadian military authorities for the allocation of another infantry brigade for 5 Cdn Armd Div.

3. After careful consideration I have come to the definite conclusion that the need for a second infantry brigade in each armoured division will continue throughout any operations that the Allied Armies in Italy may be called upon to undertake during the present was against Germany. Representations have already been made to Field Marshal Smuts for a coloured infantry brigade to be provided for 6 S.A. Armd Div. The Field Marshal as replied that he wished the matter to stand over till his return. Even if he then agrees

it will take some time to bring a coloured brigade to Italy and train it to operate with 6 S.A. Armd Div. Meanwhile it is operationally essential for 24 Gds Bde to remain attached to 6 S.A. Armd Div, and in any case it would be extremely useful to have a spare infantry brigade for attachment to armoured divisions as required in relief of a depleted brigade. This means that 24 Gds Bde will not now be available to rejoin 1 Inf Div which must in consequence retain 18 Inf Bde to maintain three infantry brigades. This in turn means that there would not even be one infantry brigade for 1 Armd Div, much less two. The armoured brigade of 1 Armd Div could however be very usefully retained as an independent armoured brigade.

4. I fully realise the objections that will be raised to the disbandment of any formations, and particularly to the disbandment of 1 Br Armd Div, but in view of the acute manpower position, and the fact that for the reasons given above there is no prospect of this formation being required to function as a division, I can see no alternative. I therefore recommend:-

(a) That 1Br Armd Div be disbanded
(b) That 2 Armd Bde becomes an independent armd bde
(c) That 18 Inf Bde remains in 1 Inf Div
(d) That any regular, or long standing T.A. units among the divisional troops be placed in other formations at my discretion.
(e) That any other divisional troops units be disbanded and the personnel used as reinforcements.

5. I propose that 24 Gds Bde shall remain attached to 6 S.A. Armd Div unless a coloured bde is provided, when 24 Gds Bde would become an independent infantry brigade and be utilised to relieve depleted brigades as required.

6. As regards 61 Inf Bde I most strongly recommend for the reasons stated in para 1 above, it should be recognised as a permanent war time institution, and as a regular component of 6 Br Armd Div.

7. I should be grateful for the earliest possible information whether my recommendations are accepted, and for early authority to put them into effect. I have given this matter very careful thought, and can see no other solution to the problem that would not involve a continued waste of manpower, or loss of over-all fighting efficiency in several formations, either of which would be fatal at this stage of the war.

8. I should also be most grateful of you would support the request of Comd 1 Cdn Corps, which he made direct to the Canadian military authorities, for a second infantry brigade for 5 Cdn Armd Div.

/s/H.R. Alexander
General
Commander-in-Chief

Sketch maps

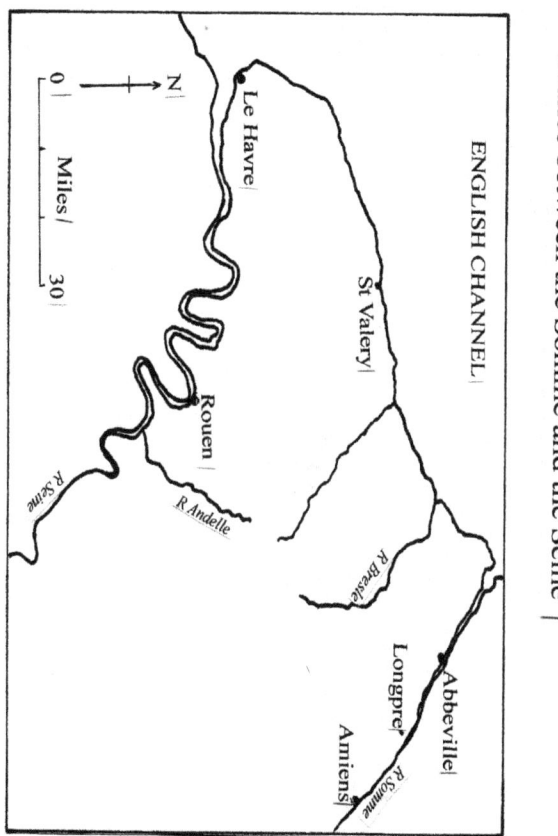

Sketch 1
France between the Somme and the Seine

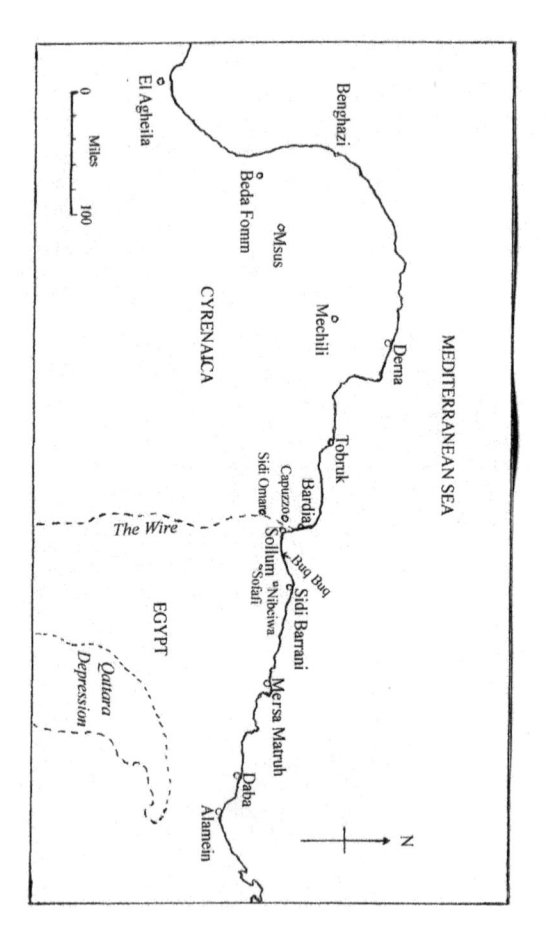

Sketch 2
The Desert

Sketch 3 THE RETREAT TO GAZALA

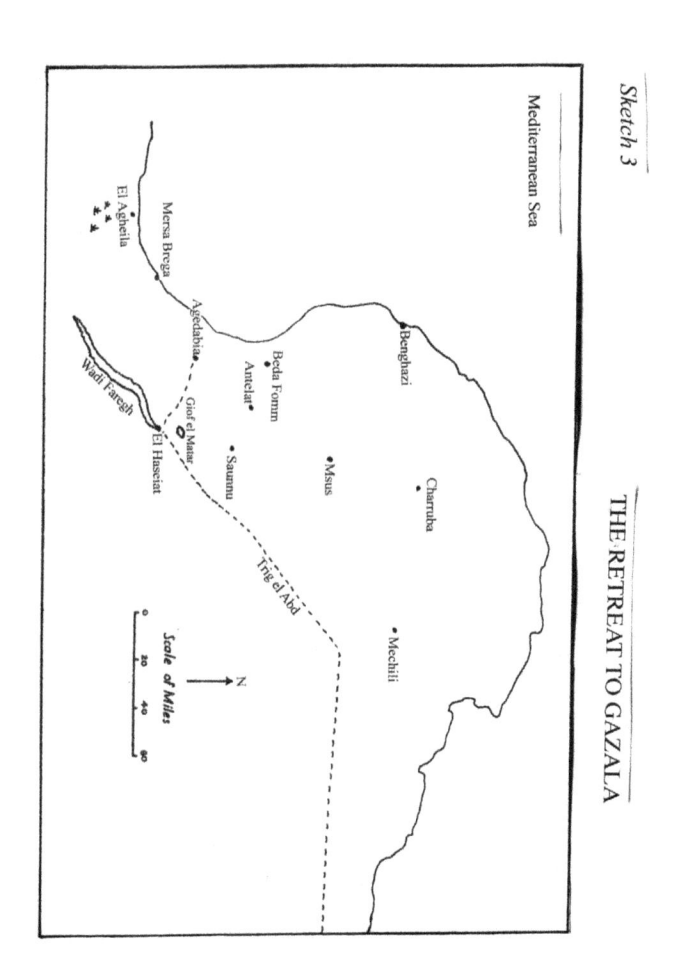

Sketch 4
The Gazala Battlefield

Sketch 5

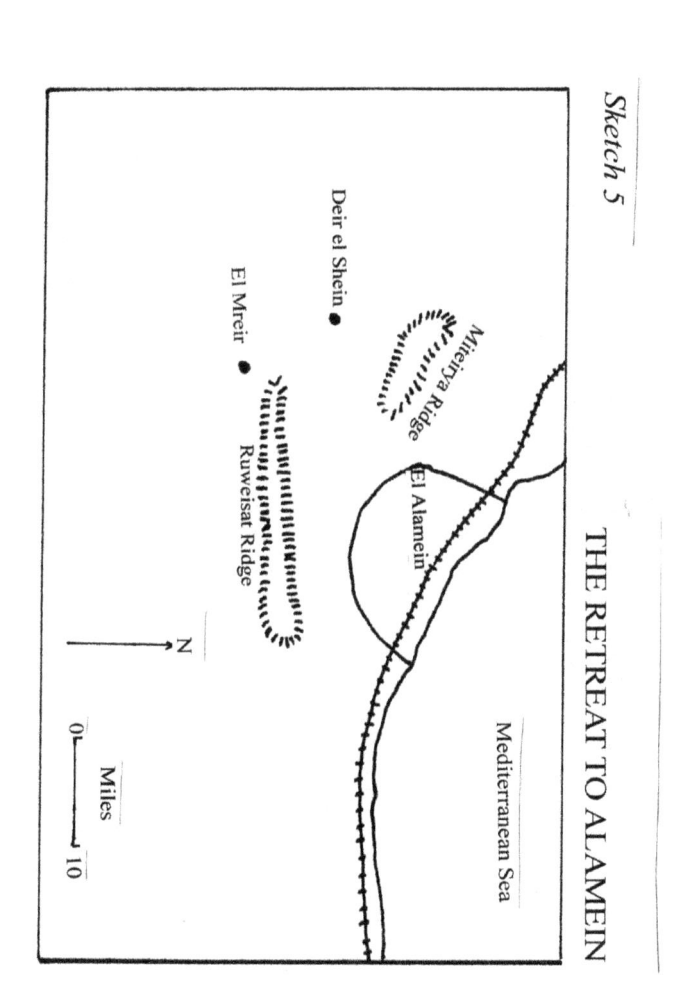

THE RETREAT TO ALAMEIN

Sketch 6 THE GOTHIC LINE

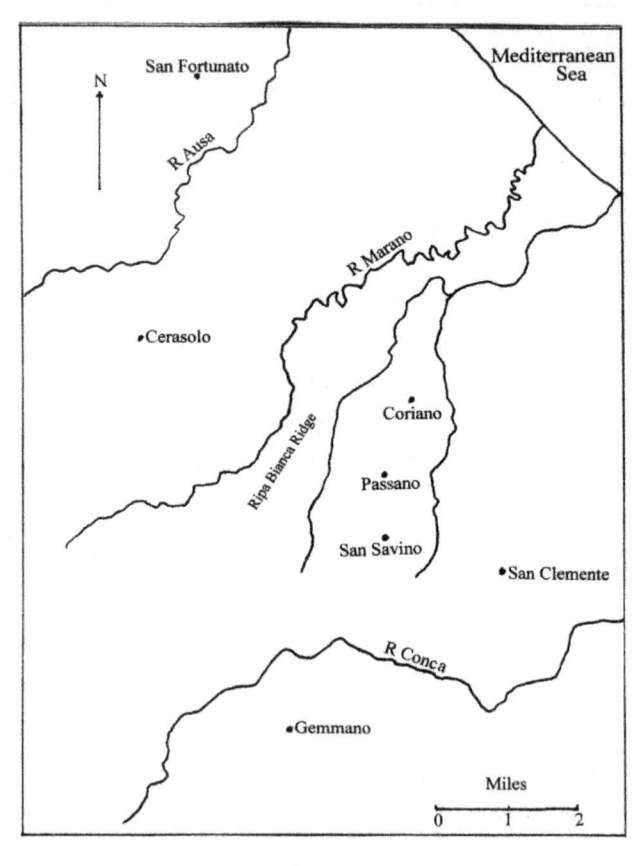